# MEETINGS THAT WORK

## About the Author:

Alexander Strauch has served as a teacher and pastor elder at the Littleton Bible Chapel in Littleton, Colorado, for more than thirty years. He and his wife, Marilyn, have four children and two grandchildren.

Other books by Alexander Strauch include:

*Biblical Eldership:*
*An Urgent Call to Restore Biblical Church Leadership*

*Study Guide to Biblical Eldership:*
*Twelve Lessons for Mentoring Men for Eldership*

*The Mentor's Guide to Biblical Eldership:*
*Twelve Lessons for Mentoring Men for Eldership*
(coauthored with Richard Swartley)

*The New Testament Deacon:*
*Minister of Mercy*

*The New Testament Deacon:*
*Study Guide*

*The Hospitality Commands:*
*Building Loving Christian Community;*
*Building Bridges to Friends and Neighbors*

*Agape Leadership:*
*Lessons in Spiritual Leadership from the Life of R. C. Chapman*
(coauthored with Robert L. Peterson)

*Men and Women:*
*Equal Yet Different*

# MEETINGS THAT WORK

## A GUIDE TO EFFECTIVE ELDERS' MEETINGS

LEWIS AND ROTH PUBLISHERS
Littleton, Colorado 80160-0569 U.S.A.

Library of Congress Cataloging-in-Publication Data

Strauch, Alexander, 1944–
Meetings that work : a guide to effective elders' meetings / Alexander Strauch.
p. cm.
Includes bibliographical references and index.
ISBN 0-936083-17-4
1. Elders (Church officers) 2. Church meeetings. I. Title.
BV680.S77 2001
254'.6—dc21 2001029996

Editor: Amanda Sorenson
Cover design: Eric Anderson
Typography: Shannon Wingrove

Printed in the United States of America

08 07 06 05 04 03 02 8 7 6 5 4 3

# Contents

# Introduction

**WHILE I WAS STANDING** at the rear of the church sanctuary where I had just finished preaching, I overheard a disturbing conversation. Three of the church elders were deciding on a time to have their next elders' meeting. One insisted that he was too busy to meet any time soon. Another suggested that their business could be accomplished easily in less than ten minutes. The others happily agreed with his assessment, so while everyone else was talking or leaving, the elders had a quick, stand-up meeting at the back of the sanctuary.

It didn't seem to occur to these men that they had allocated no time for prayer to seek God's guidance on their decisions. It didn't seem to matter that they were neglecting their pastoral work of greeting and ministering to the people after the service. Mercifully, God didn't strike them dead for their pastoral indifference as He did the careless priests Nadab and Abihu.[1] But within a few years, their church was nearly dead.

Although this degree of disinterest in elders' meetings is extreme, it illustrates the prevailing indifference that many elders have toward meetings. Mack Tennyson, author of *Making Committees Work,* humorously comments, "To write good things about meetings is almost like speaking well of Adolf Hitler. Everyone loves to bad-mouth meetings. No one speaks well of them. Most people see them as evil."[2]

**Mercifully, God didn't strike them dead for their pastoral indifference. But within a few years, their church was nearly dead.**

As much as they may dislike meetings, most elders realize that they need to meet together as a group because church eldership is shared leadership. But most elders fail to understand the profound importance of their meetings. They fail to recognize the impact their meetings have on themselves and on every aspect of the life of the local congregation. So my purpose in writing this book is twofold:

First, I wish to explain why elders' meetings are vitally important. Much more takes place in elders' meetings than merely discussing finances and programs. Meetings refine character, build group morale, provide pastoral accountability, sharpen pastoral skills, clarify doctrine, generate vision, and ignite the power of prayer. Also, elders' meetings provide a training ground for future elders.

**Many elders are tired of attending tedious, aimless, unproductive meetings.**

Second, I want to help elders improve the effectiveness of their meetings. Many elders are tired of attending tedious, aimless, unproductive meetings. By nature, meetings can be stressful, but for a meeting to be unproductive is a double frustration. Moreover, God's flock suffers if the shepherds are ineffective in their work. So I have provided numerous guidelines for conducting an effective meeting. In addition, this book, although it is written primarily for church elders, can be adapted readily by deacons or other church committees to improve the quality of their meetings.

Meetings don't have to be boring timewasters. Frustrating, tiresome, inefficient meetings can be transformed into spiritually productive and personally satisfying meetings. This book presents biblical principles and practical suggestions that can help to:

- Stimulate your God-given creativity, so that you can develop improvements that suit your local church situation
- Challenge you to continually evaluate and improve your meetings
- Improve your team management and communication skills
- Facilitate needed change
- Apply God's Word to your meetings and your work
- Place Christ at the center of your meetings

Part Three of this book (p. 65) provides questions and assignments that will help your group evaluate its meeting strengths and weaknesses and identify areas for improvement. It offers a step-by-step plan for discussing and implementing the suggestions in this book.

Throughout this book are suggested biblical texts to memorize. Please take these Scripture memory assignments seriously because they will help you become a better shepherd and meeting participant. God's Word needs to be imbedded in our minds and hearts so that it will guide our conduct, attitudes, and actions during the course of our meetings. Our goal is to have Christ-centered meetings that glorify God and result in better pastoral care of His flock.

*Part One*

# The Importance of Elders' Meetings

**FROM THE BOOK OF EXODUS** to the Epistle of James, we learn that God's people have always had a council of elders (the presbytery) to lead them. Even around the throne of God, there is a heavenly council of elders (Rev. 4:4). The New Testament teaches that Christian eldership is pastoral leadership by a council of qualified, Spirit-appointed men. It defines Christian elders as shepherds, overseers, stewards, and leaders of the local church. It also models and teaches the plurality of elders. (See Appendix A: Equality and Diversity within the Eldership, p. 69.)

Elders act as a body, a council, a team. As a team, they lead the church. A significant part of their work can be accomplished only by meeting together as a council. The verses below reveal what the New Testament says about elders and their work. These verses are absolutely foundational to understanding the rest of this book.

> "And this [the church in Antioch] did, sending [the offering] in charge of Barnabas and Saul to the elders" (Acts 11:30).

> "[Paul and Barnabas] ... appointed elders for them in every church" (Acts 14:23*a*).

> "The apostles and the elders came together to look into this [doctrinal] matter" (Acts 15:6).

> "From Miletus he [Paul] sent to Ephesus and called to him the elders of the church [and said to them...], 'Be on guard for yourselves and for all the flock, among which the Holy Spirit has made you overseers, to shepherd [pastor] the church of God which He purchased with His own blood. I know that after my departure savage wolves will come in among you, not sparing the flock; and from among your own selves men will arise, speaking perverse things, to draw away the disciples after them. Therefore be on the alert [for false teachers]'" (Acts 20:17, 28-31*a*).

"To all the saints in Christ Jesus who are in Philippi, including the overseers and deacons" (Phil. 1:1*b*).

"But we request of you, brethren, that you appreciate those who diligently labor among you, and have charge over you in the Lord and give you instruction" (1 Thess. 5:12).

"It is a trustworthy statement: If any man aspires to the office of overseer, it is a fine work he desires to do. An overseer [elder], then, must be above reproach, the husband of one wife … hospitable, able to teach, … not a new convert, so that he will not become conceited and fall into the condemnation incurred by the devil. And he must have a good reputation with those outside the church, so that he will not fall into reproach and the snare of the devil" (1 Tim. 3:1-7).

"Do not neglect the spiritual gift within you, which was bestowed on you through prophetic utterance with the laying on of hands by the presbytery [the council of elders]" (1 Tim. 4:14).

"The elders who rule well are to be considered worthy of double honor, especially those who work hard at preaching and teaching. For the Scripture says, 'You shall not muzzle the ox while he is threshing,' and 'The laborer is worthy of his wages.' Do not receive an accusation against an elder except on the basis of two or three witnesses. Those who continue in sin, rebuke in the presence of all.… Do not lay hands upon anyone [new or restored elder] too hastily and thereby share responsibility for the sins of others; keep yourself free from sin.… The sins of some men [elder candidates] are quite evident, going before them to judgment; for others, their sins follow after. Likewise also, deeds that are good are quite evident, and those which are otherwise cannot be concealed" (1 Tim. 5:17-25).

"For this reason I left you in Crete, that you would set in order what remains and appoint elders in every city as I directed you, namely, if any man is above reproach.… For the overseer must be above reproach as *God's steward,* … holding fast the faithful word which is in accordance with the teaching, so that he will be *able both to exhort in sound doctrine and to refute those who contradict*" (Titus 1:5-9; italics added).

"Obey your leaders [plural] and submit to them, for they keep watch over your souls as those who will give an account" (Heb. 13:17).

"Is anyone among you sick? Then he must call for the elders of the church and they are to pray over him, anointing him with oil in the name of the Lord; and the prayer offered in faith will restore the one who is sick, and the Lord will raise him up, and if he has committed sins, they will be forgiven him" (James 5:14,15).

📖 "Therefore, I [Peter] exhort the elders among you, … *shepherd* [pastor] *the flock of God* among you, exercising oversight not under compulsion, but voluntarily, according to the will of God; and not for sordid gain, but with eagerness; *nor yet as lording it over those allotted to your charge,* but proving to be examples to the flock. And when the Chief Shepherd appears, you will receive the unfading crown of glory. You younger men, likewise, be subject to your elders; and all of you, clothe yourselves with humility toward one another, for God is opposed to the proud, but gives grace to the humble" (1 Peter 5:1-5; italics added).

**Unfortunately, many elders do not understand the full significance of their meetings, nor do they understand the impact their meetings have on themselves and the congregation.**

Pastoral leadership by a council of elders obviously requires elders to meet together regularly. So meetings are an indispensable feature of the elders' work. Meetings have an important function that cannot be replaced by anything else. Unfortunately, many elders don't understand the full significance of their meetings, nor do they understand the impact their meetings have on themselves and the congregation. Thoughtfully consider the following reasons why elders' meetings are important.

## MEETINGS AFFECT THE SPIRITUAL HEALTH OF THE FLOCK

The eldership is the church's principal leadership and decision-making council. So the elders' meetings are multifaceted meetings that involve problem solving, decision making, coordination of church activities, information sharing, brainstorming, study, planning, and fervent prayer. According to the New Testament, the elders jointly:

- Shepherd the flock (1 Peter 5:2)
- Oversee the flock (1 Peter 5:2)
- Lead the people (1 Tim. 5:17; 1 Thess. 5:12)

- Manage the household of God (Titus 1:7)
- Investigate and judge doctrinal matters (Acts 15:6; Titus 1:9; 2:1)
- Dispense counsel (Acts 21:17-26)

So in a real sense the elders' meetings are the critical nerve center of the local church body.

> **A clear connection exists between the quality of the elders' meetings and the quality of the elders' pastoral leadership.**

Make no mistake about it, elders' meetings affect the spiritual health of the church. What elders talk about, what they do or don't do, how they act toward one another, and what they plan or fail to plan affects every member of the flock. Thus a clear connection exists between the quality of the elders' meetings and the quality of the elders' pastoral leadership.

If the meetings are headed nowhere, if they are unproductive, if they deal only with facilities and finances, and if they have little spiritual life, the flock will feel the sad effects. Elders, too, will experience the frustration of wasted time and effort. In an effective elders' meeting, on the other hand, godly decisions are reached, direction is given, problems are identified and solved, plans are refined and improved upon, vision is cast, sins are confronted, error is brought to light, and pastoral vigilance is enhanced. The result is better spiritual care for the flock by a more dynamic eldership team.

> **Elders' meetings provide a model for every committee and leadership team in the church.**

Furthermore, the elder council is a microcosm of how the whole congregation should live and work together. Elders' meetings provide a model for every committee and leadership team in the church. As elders work together according to biblical principles, they demonstrate the Christlike life of service, love, unity, forbearance, humility, prayer, and doctrinal faithfulness. Their behavior and attitudes set the tone for the entire church community.

People want good leadership. They desire to be cared for, protected, fed, challenged, and given fresh vision and new ideas. So don't disappoint them. Provide the godly leadership and care they need and crave. Start by taking control of your meetings so that they center on spiritual leadership and pastoral care.

## MEETINGS BUILD CHARACTER

There are no graduates from Christ's school of shepherding. We all have much to learn about becoming like the Good Shepherd who gave His life for the sheep (John 10:11-13). We all need to improve our:

- Love and compassion for people
- Wisdom and counsel
- Ability to lovingly confront people and issues
- Sensitivity in dealing with complaints and questions
- Prayer life

Although all elders must be morally and spiritually qualified before serving as pastor elders, they are still imperfect human beings, sinners saved by grace. They have weaknesses, character flaws, imperfect skills, annoying eccentricities, blind spots, and imbalances that need improvement. These imperfections at times make working together painfully difficult. Under the pressure of meetings, pride, bad tempers, lack of love, poor people skills, or a controlling spirit are exposed and cry out for correction. Under the same circumstances, strength of character and abilities are also revealed and become a blessing to all.

The goal of every shepherd is to become more like the Good Shepherd, the Lord Jesus Christ, and elders' meetings help develop Christlike character. God has used the elders' meetings to expose the weaknesses of my character and to reshape it into a more Christlike character. Mack Tennyson aptly expresses this truth:

> Meetings provide a good place to practice the Christianity we preach. The Christian fruits are love, joy, peace, patience, kindness, goodness, faithfulness, gentleness, and self-control (Gal. 5:22-23). Faking these fruits for a church service or a church fellowship dinner or when working for the poor is easy. But faking them in church meetings is hard. The next time you feel that you are wasting time in a meeting, think about the character you are developing.[1]

An elder with a teachable spirit will soon discover elders' meetings to be a sort of graduate school for developing Spirit-controlled character. Being a pastor elder stretches one's mind, character, knowledge of the Bible, prayer life, and people skills to the limit. Each meeting tests one's love, self-control, forgiveness, humility, truthfulness, knowledge of the Word, spiritual wisdom, and pastoral skills.

By having to deal with tough questions and agonizing life problems, elders are forced to study and apply God's Word like they have never done before. They are also forced to pray like they have never prayed before.

During my first year as a pastor elder, for example, one of the elders and I would go to a restaurant after our meetings. Over a cup of coffee, my friend would tactfully point out my shortcomings that had been exhibited during the meeting. He would say things like, "You don't listen as well as you should," "You need to speak more gently," or "You scare the older men with all your ideas." At times it was discouraging to hear of my repeated failures, but nonetheless I invited my friend to keep helping me improve. These times together were life-changing experiences that proved essential to my maturing in Christlike leadership skills.

**Each meeting tests one's love, self-control, forgiveness, humility, truthfulness, knowledge of the Word, spiritual wisdom, and pastoral skills.**

Meetings truly are a spiritual workshop in which God refines one's character, and in Christian work character is everything.

## MEETINGS DEVELOP LEADERSHIP SKILLS AND GODLY WISDOM

Meetings provide on-the-job training for developing pastoral leadership skills and godly wisdom. Each elder (assuming he is biblically qualified) has unique wisdom and skills to contribute to the group and to teach others. As elders meet and work together, they teach one another and learn from one another. King Solomon expressed the kind of mutual growth that one can expect from participating with a council of elders when he wrote, "Iron sharpens iron, so one man sharpens another" (Prov. 27:17). Commenting on this verse in his classic commentary on Proverbs, Charles Bridges writes, "[As] steel whetted against a knife sharpens the edge, so the collision of different minds whets each the edge of the other."[2]

The dynamic interaction that takes place during an elders' meeting sharpens a person's mind and communication skills. It is impossible to participate in an intense, highly interactive meeting that involves difficult church problems without growing in biblical wisdom and improving one's pastoral skills and knowledge of doctrine. This kind of human interaction and learning cannot come from a book or a computer; it must be experienced. So elders need to understand that each meeting, despite how frustrating or unproductive it may seem, is a learning opportunity.

Active participation in meetings, moreover, sharpens an elder's leadership skills and ability to give wise counsel. Also, one or more of the elders may have exceptional wisdom and years of rich pastoral experience that can be an invaluable aid to helping others grow in their pastoral skills. The Bible tells us, "He who walks with wise men will be wise" (Prov. 13:20). As newer, inexperienced elders watch experienced elders care for people, deal with difficult people, and make wise group decisions, they will learn by example—a thoroughly biblical way of learning and of teaching others.[3] Meetings, then, are a school for continual improvement of one's:

- Teamwork
- Communication skills
- Tact with people
- Personal organization
- Leadership abilities
- Competence in counseling
- Shepherding skills

## MEETINGS ENHANCE GROUP MORALE AND ACCOUNTABILITY

We need to remember that people are more important than meetings. So an eldership team needs to develop the friendship-relationship aspect of eldership as well as the task-organizational aspect. An eldership team that is solely work-oriented is imbalanced. It is missing out on loving relationships, a key element of a healthy church leadership team.

Elders must actively work at building a community spirit by genuinely caring for one another and becoming Christlike servants to one another. Leading God's people isn't easy. Elders are busy people who are engaged in frontline spiritual warfare. Listening to complaints and dealing with people's sins wear a person down. Even Moses fell apart under the pressure of the people's sins and complaints (Num. 11:10-15). The friendlier and closer that elders are to one another, the better prepared they are to handle the pressure and disagreements that occur while leading a church.

The elders' meetings provide a regular social setting in which elders can encourage and enjoy fellowship with one another. Meetings provide a regular forum for sharing personal needs and prayer requests. Praying for one another binds people together, enhancing their knowledge of and pastoral care for one another. Meetings also provide an opportunity for elders to acknowledge and thank one another for special efforts or faithfulness to a task. Paul delighted in acknowledging and thanking God for his fellow laborers, and Barnabas is known as a minister of encouragement (Acts 4:36; 11:22-24). The ministry of encouragement is a powerful, rewarding ministry that is much needed in our churches today.[4] So seek to be a team of elders that continually encourages and thanks God for one another.

**Elders must actively work at building a community spirit by genuinely caring for one another and becoming Christlike servants to one another.**

Moreover, meetings allow elders time to counsel and admonish one another. We must not forget that each elder is under the pastoral authority and care of the entire eldership body. The eldership is responsible for caring for the welfare of each elder and his family. This includes being genuinely concerned for the spiritual condition of the elder, his wife, and his children. At times an elder council may need to advise an elder to pull back from some responsibilities because of an overloaded work schedule or a stressful home situation. In practical ways like this, elders guard one another's souls; they act as loving pastors to one another.

Finally, and of crucial concern, elders' meetings provide an official forum for accountability. Genuine accountability helps elders (as well as others) become better stewards of their time and gifts. It helps protect them from the all-too-common human tendencies toward procrastination, laziness, misdirectedness, and forgetfulness. This is one reason Jesus sent His disciples out by twos (Mark 6:7; Luke 10:1).

**Don't fear group accountability—welcome it; seek it.**

Eldership is nothing if it does not include genuine group accountability. Regular reporting and answering to one another help elders fulfill their pastoral duties. As a team member, each elder is answerable to the group for his actions. If an elder is having difficulty fulfilling his duties, this can be openly discussed and the group can provide counsel and assistance to relieve the problem. So don't fear group accountability—welcome it; seek it. The eldership will be the better for it.

## MEETINGS TRAIN FUTURE ELDERS

Part of the responsibility of overseeing God's flock involves preparing future shepherds in order to provide for the ongoing leadership of the church. Elders cannot afford to be passive about this matter. Paul charged Timothy to identify and train men who were trustworthy in character and capable of teaching. "The things which you have heard from me," he wrote, "entrust these to faithful men who will be able to teach others also" (2 Tim. 2:2). This is a beautiful description of a qualified, biblical elder.

These words are as urgently needed today as when Paul wrote them to Timothy. Elders need to develop a shepherd's eye for identifying men of trustworthy character (Titus 1:6-8) and teaching ability (Titus 1:9-13), and they need to have a practical plan of action for both challenging and training potential pastor elders. Kenneth O. Gangel reminds us of this simple, but fundamental truth: "The key to reproducing leadership is to clearly plan for it."[5] "Church leaders," he goes on to say, "need to produce leaders who will reproduce leaders precisely as it is done in the family—through experience, instruction, and modeling."[6]

One practical way to challenge potential elders is by inviting them to attend elders' meetings as observers. This allows them to learn firsthand about pastoral care. Indeed, no one should be appointed an elder if he has not spent time observing elders' meetings and learning to work with the eldership council.

Many of the skills needed to shepherd a congregation are learned best by watching and doing. The best way to teach potential elders how to pray for people, for example, is to have them pray regularly with the elders. As they pray with the elders about the many needs of the people, they will get to know the people and experience the elders' heart for the people.

**Elders need to have a practical plan of action for both challenging and training potential pastor elders.**

Also, elders need to learn how to work with others as a team of servants. They need to submit to one another, to wait patiently on one another, to love and forgive, to be open and truthful, and to recognize and repent of deep-seated pride and selfish independence (Phil. 2:3,4). People in Western cultures value individuality, rugged independence, self-determination, and equality, so it's not surprising that good team cooperation doesn't come naturally to most of us. We learn the skills of servanthood best through the consistent, and at times difficult, hands-on experience of being part of a leadership team.

**Our Lord never trained any man alone. He called and trained men as a team.**

Of course, preparing for eldership involves more than exposure to meetings. Doctrinal and pastoral training is essential for preparing future elders. Nevertheless, a vital part of that training should include attending and observing elders' meetings. Our Lord never trained any man alone. He called and trained men as a team. He devoted a major portion of His life and time to training a team of twelve men. As A. B. Bruce, in his classic volume *The Training of the Twelve,* observes:

> Both from His words and from His actions we can see that He attached supreme importance to that part of His work which consisted in training the twelve. In the intercessory prayer [John 17:6], e.g., He speaks of the training He had given these men as if it had been the principal part of His own earthly ministry. And such, in one sense, it really was. The careful, painstaking education of the disciples secured that the Teacher's influence on the world should be permanent.[7]

Oh, that local church elders might have such a passion for training others!

Let us never underestimate the significance of the elders' meetings. Elders' meetings should be a time of refining character, sharpening leadership skills, training younger elders, challenging potential elders, seeking God through group prayer, growing in the wisdom and knowledge of God's Word, enjoying rich fellowship together, and laboring on behalf of God's precious flock. As such, elders' meetings bring great blessing into our lives. In his book *The Team Concept,* Bruce Stabbert tells of the blessings he has experienced as a result of being part of a biblical eldership team. His words should be an encouragement to make our elders' meetings all they can be:

> They [the elders] are responsible for guiding the church people by making wise decisions and by careful administration. To do this, they must be humble men of prayer. They must be conscious of sound principles of management and decision making. They must not be impulsive or dictatorial, but rather cautious and concerned for the feelings of the church. This requires that the elders meet together at least weekly, in order to pray together and superintend church life. Our elders meet on Monday nights from seven to eleven or twelve. These times have been some of the greatest hours in my life, to sit among Spirit-filled men who are humbly seeking Christ's direction for the church. There is every prospect that men of diverse perspectives will be able to lead together with a blessed unity, if they submit themselves one to the other in the fear of Christ. (Eph. 5:21) [8]

*Part Two*

# Helps for Achieving Effective Elders' Meetings

**ELDERS SPEND MANY HOURS** attending meetings. I, for example, spend a minimum of one hundred hours a year in elders' meetings. Over the years I have spent more than three thousand hours in elders' meetings. This is in addition to time spent in related meetings. Unfortunately, not all of this time has been productive.

My experience is not unique. Despite the many hours elders spend in meetings, most have never been taught how to conduct productive, satisfying meetings. Here are some frequently heard complaints:

- Too much time is spent discussing facility or financial issues rather than spiritual matters.
- There is inadequate prayer time.
- Participants drift off the subject and fail to stay on track when discussing important issues.
- The group gets tied up in trivial, irrelevant matters and fails to reach conclusions.
- Inadequate thought is given to meeting preparation.
- There is poor follow-up on decisions and tasks.
- The group fails to follow an agenda, so meetings drag on with little accomplished.
- Certain people talk too much.

The fact is, elders have to learn how to conduct good meetings and how to participate effectively. The ideas and biblical principles presented in the following pages can significantly improve the elders' meetings and individual participation in them.

There may, however, be disagreement about how to implement some of these ideas, so be patient with and understanding of one another. Remember the words of our Lord Jesus Christ to His team of strident disciples: "Have salt in yourselves, and be at peace with one another" (Mark 9:50).

## BIBLICALLY QUALIFIED PARTICIPANTS

First, and of primary significance, effective meetings require the right participants—those whom the Holy Spirit has chosen (Acts 20:28). God is supremely concerned about who leads His flock and who sits on the elder council. Thus the Holy Spirit lays down specific, objective character and ability requirements for elders. These qualifications protect the church from unfit men and set a standard by which elders may continually measure themselves.

> **Despite the many hours elders spend in meetings, most have never been taught how to conduct productive, satisfying meetings. . . . The fact is, elders have to learn how to conduct good meetings and how to participate effectively.**

Scripture further requires that a potential candidate for eldership be examined as to his fitness regarding the qualifications (1 Tim. 3:10; 5:22-25). Tragically, many churches never examine their candidates according to the biblical requirements. The failure to examine candidates is a major source of problems and ineffectiveness within the eldership and also impairs the spiritual growth of the church.

> **Effective meetings require the right participants—those whom the Holy Spirit has chosen (Acts 20:28).**

The biblical qualifications for an elder are listed in 1 Timothy 3: 1-7, Titus 1:5-9, and 1 Peter 5:1-4. From these passages, I have chosen eleven characteristics that are especially important if a person is to be a good meeting participant and decision maker.[1] Take a few minutes to be sure you undertand the meaning and importance of each.

**Gentle:** forbearing, patient, graciously amenable, yielding wherever yielding is possible

**Temperate:** self-controlled, balanced in judgment, free from debilitating excesses or rash behavior

**Sensible:** sound-minded, discreet, able to keep an objective perspective in the face of problems and disagreements

**Not pugnacious:** not a fighter, bad-tempered, or irritable

**Not a new convert:** not someone who is inexperienced or spiritually immature

**Peaceable:** not quarrelsome

**Not self-willed:** not arrogant and inconsiderate of others' opinions, feelings, or desires

**Not quick-tempered:** not a "hothead" or an angry man

**Just:** a righteous, law-abiding man of principle

**Not domineering or authoritarian:** willing to listen and yield to others

**Sound in doctrine:** able to teach and to refute false teaching

A person with these character qualities will work well on an eldership team. His balanced judgment will be an asset in conducting meetings and making decisions, and his self-control will enable him to work well with others.

Unfit or unqualified elders will prove to be a hindrance to the effectiveness of the elders' meetings and to the elders' overall leadership. So the first step to effective meetings is to appoint none other than biblically qualified, Spirit-appointed elders.

## BIBLICAL GROUND RULES OF CONDUCT FOR MEETINGS

Meetings are a good place to discover whether we really think and act according to the ways of Jesus Christ. Paul wrote, "Therefore I exhort you, be imitators of me. For this reason I have sent to you Timothy ... and he will remind you of *my ways which are in Christ,* just as I teach everywhere in every church" (1 Cor. 4:16,17; italics added). Spiritually rewarding meetings are the result of each participant being fully committed to practicing biblical principles of conduct and Christlike attitudes.

Don't forget this vital biblical truth: Christ is present at all our meetings (Matt. 18:20). Each participant is to conduct himself in a manner worthy of the gospel (Phil. 1:27). Elders' meetings should be characterized by the presence, leadership, and control of Jesus Christ through the Holy Spirit, not the flesh. Temper tantrums, angry outbursts of emotion, the "silent treatment," manipulation, threatening talk, or derogatory accusations are unacceptable behavior in any meeting that is conducted in Christ's name.

Elders need to be keenly aware that each participant's attitude and behavior affect the quality of a meeting. There are right and wrong ways to talk to one another, disagree with one another, reason with one another, press one another for change, and persuade. Sinful attitudes produce unpleasant meetings; godly attitudes produce joyous meetings. So let us consider the conduct that should characterize all those who meet in Christ's name to do Christ's business.

**Spiritually rewarding meetings are the result of each participant being fully committed to practicing biblical principles of conduct and Christlike attitudes.**

## Conduct Yourself with a Christlike Attitude

For Christians, the popular saying "attitude is everything" must be taken one step further: "*Christ*'s attitude is everything." Philippians 2:5 provides the fundamental ground rule for all meetings: "Have this attitude in yourselves which was also in Christ Jesus." Christ's attitude of humility and self-sacrifice should permeate every meeting and shape the attitude of every participant. Although Jesus Christ existed in the form of God, He "did not regard equality with God a thing to be grasped, but emptied Himself, taking the form of a bond-servant.... He humbled Himself by becoming obedient to the point of death, even death on a cross" (Phil. 2:6-8).

Our teacher and Lord was humble and selfless. He was never proud or self-seeking. As a result of His example of humility and self-giving, Paul wrote, "Do nothing from selfishness or empty conceit, but with humility of mind regard one another as more important than yourselves; do not merely look out for your own personal interests, but also for the interests of others" (Phil. 2:3,4). So in the process of discussion and decision making, our attitude should always be Christ's attitude of humility and selflessness. The spirit of our meetings should be one of humbly washing one another's feet (John 13:12-15), not chopping off one another's heads!

The deceitful sins of pride and selfishness ruin any hope for peaceful group cooperation. "But if you have bitter jealousy and selfish ambition in your heart," James writes, "do not be arrogant and so lie against the truth. This wisdom is not that which comes down from above, but is earthly, natural, demonic. For where jealousy and selfish ambition exist, there is disorder and every evil thing" (James 3:14-16). So before you speak, check your attitude. Is it Christ's attitude or the devil's?

**The spirit of our meetings should be one of humbly washing one another's feet, not chopping off one another's heads!**

Examine your attitudes and your behavior in light of the following verses:

- "You call Me Teacher and Lord; and you are right, for so I am. If I then, the Lord and the Teacher, washed your feet, you also ought to wash one another's feet. For I gave you an example that you also should do as I did to you" (John 13:14,15).
- "Give preference to one another in honor" (Rom. 12:10*b*).
- "Let us not become boastful, challenging one another, envying one another" (Gal. 5:26).

*Scripture Memory Assignment:*
*Philippians 2:3-9*

## Conduct Yourself with Christlike Love

The "new commandment" directly from our Lord Jesus Christ sets the standard of conduct for all meetings: "A new commandment I give to you, that you love one another, *even as I have loved you,* that you also love one another. By this all men will know that you are My disciples, if you have love for one another" (John 13:34,35; italics added).

In a real sense, every meeting is a test of our growth in Christlike love. Without love, elders at best merely tolerate one another; at worst, they sabotage each other. Love helps us overcome our fears of one another's differences, understand one another better, disagree with grace, be less defensive and more open to others' ideas, listen better, cooperate more, take more risks, fight less, and forgive the hurts we all unintentionally inflict on one another in the course of intense interaction. In the uncomfortable heat of human conflict, only love "covers" (1 Peter 4:8).

The "more excellent way," the Christian way of life (1 Cor. 12:31), sets the ground rules for all our meetings: "Let all that you do [even meetings] be done in love" (1 Cor. 16:14). In order to more fully understand Christlike love, read and then apply Paul's great love chapter to yourself as an elder:

> "[An elder] is patient, … is kind and is not jealous.… [An elder] does not brag.… [An elder] is not arrogant, does not act unbecomingly … does not seek [his] own, … is not provoked, does not take into account a wrong suffered, does not rejoice in unrighteousness, but rejoices with the truth; [an elder] bears all things, believes all things, hopes all things, endures all things." (1 Cor. 13:4-7)

Let us recommit ourselves to treating one another with brotherly, Christlike love. The following Scriptures are important reminders of how we are to love:

- 🕮 "Be devoted to one another in brotherly love" (Rom. 12:10*a*).
- 🕮 "Love … does not seek its own" (1 Cor. 13:4,5).
- 🕮 "With all humility and gentleness, with patience, showing tolerance for one another in love" (Eph. 4:2).
- 🕮 "Above all, keep fervent in your love for one another, because love covers a multitude of sins" (1 Peter 4:8).

*Scripture Memory Assignment:*
*John 13:34,35*

## Conduct Yourself as a Christlike Servant

In what has been called the "great reversal," Jesus Christ taught servant leadership and modeled it for His disciples: "I am among you as the one who serves" (Luke 22:27*b*). The Greeks and Romans understood leadership as "ruling over" others and as entitlement to lofty personal appellations of honor. Greatness was defined in terms of power, position, authority, and prestigious titles. Jesus, on the other hand, taught that leaders are to serve one another, to act humbly toward one another, and to live in loving brotherly community. In Christ's community, true greatness is based on service.

> And He said to them, "The kings of the Gentiles lord it over them; and those who have authority over them are called 'Benefactors.' But it is not this way with you, but the one who is the greatest among you must become like the youngest, and the leader like the servant." (Luke 22:25,26)

The servant leadership that Jesus taught and modeled also stood in opposition to that of the religious leaders who were obsessed with special privileges, status, and honorific titles. Note what Jesus said about them:

> They love the place of honor at banquets and the chief seats in the synagogues, and respectful greetings in the market places, and being called Rabbi by men. But *do not be called Rabbi*; for One is your Teacher, and *you are all brothers*.... Do not be called leaders; for One is your Leader, that is, Christ. But the greatest among you shall be your servant. Whoever exalts himself shall be humbled; and whoever humbles himself shall be exalted." (Matt. 23:6-12; italics added)

Servant leadership is a style of leadership that follows the way of the Cross (Matt. 20:28), considered by the world to be weakness and foolishness. It is a *selfless,* self-sacrificing type of leadership—most suitable for those who preach the message of the Cross and the virtues of humility, servanthood, and loving brotherhood. It is leadership that is exercised

> **Servant leadership is a selfless, self-sacrificing type of leadership most suitable for those who preach the message of the Cross and the virtues of humility, servanthood, and loving brotherhood.**

for the building up of others (2 Cor. 10:8; 13:10) and for the joy of all (2 Cor. 1:24). It willingly suffers personal humiliation and deprivation for the good of others and for the sake of the gospel (1 Cor. 4:8-13). It is leadership under the authority of Christ and His evaluation (1 Cor. 3: 10-15; 4:3-5).

Servant leadership, however, does not eliminate the exercise of leadership or authority in the church. Those with a leadership gift are exhorted by the Holy Spirit to lead with diligence and with zeal (Rom. 12:8). Gifted leaders help the elders' meetings by generating fresh ideas, providing wisdom, confronting problems, seeing future potential, and motivating the group.

Servant leadership affects not only the way elders relate to their brothers and sisters in the congregation as spiritual leaders, but the way elders treat one another when making decisions and discussing disagreeable subjects. They are to relate to one another as brethren, as servants, and with a humble spirit. They are not to play power-control games or use manipulative tactics. As elders, we need to take to heart the following verses on servant leadership:

- "Not that we lord it over your faith, but are workers with you for your joy" (2 Cor. 1:24).
- "For we do not preach ourselves but Christ Jesus as Lord, and ourselves as your bond-servants for Jesus' sake" (2 Cor. 4:5).
- "Nor yet as lording it over those allotted to your [the elders'] charge, but proving to be examples to the flock" (1 Peter 5:3).

*SCRIPTURE MEMORY ASSIGNMENT:*
*Luke 22:26,27*

## PRINCIPLES OF PERSONAL PARTICIPATION IN MEETINGS

Good meetings require good participation. People who demonstrate Christlike conduct and character will take responsibility for the success of their meetings and will seek to make constructive contributions. To have a positive influence, each meeting participant should know and practice several key principles.

### BE AN ACTIVE, RESPONSIBLE PARTICIPANT

Effective meetings result when each participant takes personal responsibility for the success, assignments, and decisions of a meeting. A responsible team member expresses his opinions and argues his points. He works diligently to help the group reach decisions. He welcomes assignments. He willingly says, "I'll make that phone call" or "I'll be glad to help with that proposal." He's concerned if one member has too many assignments while others have too few.

An inactive team member, on the other hand, keeps his head down when something needs to be done. He hopes no one will notice him or look in his direction. He resists doing more or accepting responsibility. He's an onlooker, passive and indifferent, annoyed by any extra work or time commitment.

**Effective meetings result when each participant takes personal responsibility for their success.**

To be a more active, responsible participant:

- Be involved in corporate prayer.
- Actively participate in the decision-making process.
- Be a good listener.
- Ask for clarification whenever you're unsure of what is being said.
- Always treat colleagues with Christian respect and honor.
- Help the group stick to the discussion at hand.
- If you tend to talk too much, ask another member to help you monitor this problem.
- If you tend to be a silent participant, ask another member to help you learn to express yourself more verbally.
- Maintain confidentiality; don't gossip about the group's deliberations.
- State your frustrations to your colleagues during the meeting; don't be an out-of-the-meeting complainer.
- Welcome responsibilities and assignments.
- Do your homework and research without procrastinating.
- Make the extra effort to communicate well.
- Laugh more.
- Be a problem solver, not a problem.

Scripture is clear: "Whatever you do, do your work heartily, as for the Lord rather than for men" (Col. 3:23). Whatever you do for the Lord, do it wholeheartedly. If you serve on an eldership council, serve diligently. "Whatever your hand finds to do, do it with all your might" (Eccl. 9:10).

### Be a Faithful Attender

Faithful attendance is absolutely essential to productive meetings. Absenteeism immobilizes a group. Sporadic attendance always has a negative effect on a group's morale and performance. It is frustrating when some members consistently miss meetings. In order to be a part of the eldership team, each member has made a significant investment of time and energy that should be respected. So be faithful to your commitment to your colleagues.

**Don't make your colleagues guess your whereabouts or waste their time waiting for you.**

Of course, missing a meeting is at times unavoidable, but this should be the exception, not the rule. Your fellow workers are counting on you to be present. When attendance at a meeting is impossible, the following ideas may help minimize the impact:

- Tape-record meetings so that a member who has been absent can hear what was discussed. If meetings are recorded, be sure to guard the privacy of the tapes.
- If you must miss a meeting, inform the facilitator of your absence beforehand. This shows respect for your colleagues. Don't make them guess your whereabouts or waste their time waiting for you. You are accountable to the team and your absence will be felt, so let the others know whenever you have to be absent.
- If absenteeism is a chronic problem for your eldership, openly discuss it and seek positive solutions.

## Be a Peacemaker and Unity Builder

Jesus Christ, the supreme peacemaker, said, "Blessed are the peacemakers" (Matt. 5:9). God desires that His people be at peace with one another and display unity of mind, but this is not easy to do. As a result of the Fall (Gen. 3), fighting and division plague the whole human race. Sadly, fighting and division have plagued the history of Christianity as well. Yet we must not give up. The New Testament strongly emphasizes peace and unity in the local church, beginning with the church leaders.

**Achieving unity takes much prayer, wisdom, patience, humility, and determination on the part of each elder.**

Peace and unity significantly enhance the effectiveness of the elders' work and the spiritual growth of a church. Disunity confuses, disheartens, and weakens the effectiveness of a group of elders. If it is persistent, disunity can be destructive to the church also. "If a house is divided against itself, that house will not be able to stand" (Mark 3:25). Thus each elder is to pursue peace and harmony within the church without compromising the truth of the gospel (Acts 15:1,2).

Achieving unity takes much prayer, wisdom, patience, humility, and determination on the part of each elder. To grasp the importance of peace and unity, consider the following New Testament passages:

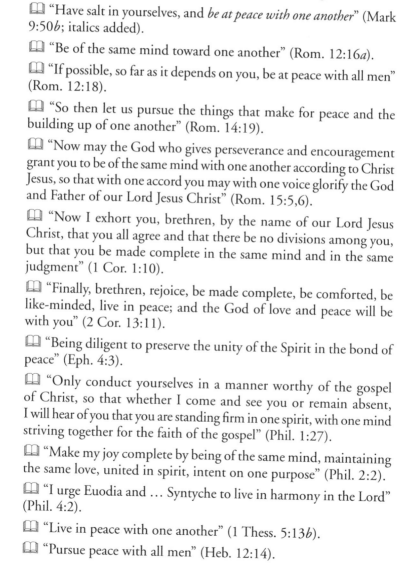

- "Have salt in yourselves, and *be at peace with one another*" (Mark 9:50*b*; italics added).
- "Be of the same mind toward one another" (Rom. 12:16*a*).
- "If possible, so far as it depends on you, be at peace with all men" (Rom. 12:18).
- "So then let us pursue the things that make for peace and the building up of one another" (Rom. 14:19).
- "Now may the God who gives perseverance and encouragement grant you to be of the same mind with one another according to Christ Jesus, so that with one accord you may with one voice glorify the God and Father of our Lord Jesus Christ" (Rom. 15:5,6).
- "Now I exhort you, brethren, by the name of our Lord Jesus Christ, that you all agree and that there be no divisions among you, but that you be made complete in the same mind and in the same judgment" (1 Cor. 1:10).
- "Finally, brethren, rejoice, be made complete, be comforted, be like-minded, live in peace; and the God of love and peace will be with you" (2 Cor. 13:11).
- "Being diligent to preserve the unity of the Spirit in the bond of peace" (Eph. 4:3).
- "Only conduct yourselves in a manner worthy of the gospel of Christ, so that whether I come and see you or remain absent, I will hear of you that you are standing firm in one spirit, with one mind striving together for the faith of the gospel" (Phil. 1:27).
- "Make my joy complete by being of the same mind, maintaining the same love, united in spirit, intent on one purpose" (Phil. 2:2).
- "I urge Euodia and … Syntyche to live in harmony in the Lord" (Phil. 4:2).
- "Live in peace with one another" (1 Thess. 5:13*b*).
- "Pursue peace with all men" (Heb. 12:14).

## Be a Person of Integrity, Not a Manipulator

Some people are so headstrong they feel justified in manipulating their brothers and sisters. But nothing is important enough to justify manipulating others. People who manipulate demean their own character, create distrust among their colleagues, ruin relationships, teach others to manipulate, give Satan a foothold, and open themselves up to further deceit.

God is holy and trustworthy, and the Christian faith is a religion of truth. In contrast, a manipulator is a distorter of truth. This world is full of lies, full of "deceitful spirits and doctrines of demons" (see 1 Tim. 4:1). This world feeds on lies and perpetuates lies, but the Lord's people are to be different. "Therefore, laying aside falsehood, speak truth each one of you with his neighbor, for we are members of one another" (Eph. 4:25; also Col. 3:9). The Lord's people are to be people of the truth and servants of the Word of truth and sound doctrine. Thus elders are to take the lead in walking in truth.

**When each participant speaks the truth openly and in love, precious mental energy is not wasted worrying about hidden agendas, backroom politicking, or destructive backbiting.**

Manipulative leadership is bad leadership. The devil is a liar and a deceiver (John 8:44). If elders feel they have to hold back pertinent information, intimidate or threaten others, tell half-truths, exaggerate, deflect legitimate questions, block honest communication, misrepresent or misquote others, shift blame, slant the facts, plot and scheme, or pout and withdraw, then they don't really believe in Christian brotherhood, love, or Christlike servanthood.

If, on the other hand, each member speaks his mind truthfully and openly, better decisions are made and brotherly relationships are preserved. When each participant speaks the truth openly and in love, precious mental energy is not wasted worrying about hidden agendas, backroom politicking, or destructive backbiting. Truthful speaking is an essential ingredient of teamwork. It builds group trust, fosters good group communication and strong community, and most important, it pleases God.

Christlike leadership, then, requires integrity of character and truthful speaking. People will follow only when they trust their leaders.

So elders need to be sure that their "yes" always means "yes" and their "no" always means "no" (2 Cor. 1:17-20).

The following Scripture passages are important reminders of the need for integrity in carrying out the Lord's work:

> 🕮 "So he [David] shepherded them according to the integrity of his heart, and guided them with his skillful hands" (Psalm 78:72).
>
> 🕮 "Lying lips are an abomination to the Lord, but those who deal faithfully [truthfully] are His delight" (Prov. 12:22).
>
> 🕮 "Righteous [honest] lips are the delight of kings, and he who speaks right [truth] is loved" (Prov. 16:13).
>
> 🕮 "Teacher [Christ], we know that You are truthful and teach the way of God in truth, and defer to no one; for You are not partial to any"(Matt. 22:16*b*).
>
> 🕮 "But the wisdom from above is *first pure,* then peaceable, gentle, reasonable, full of mercy and good fruits, unwavering, *without hypocrisy*" (James 3:17; italics added).

*SCRIPTURE MEMORY ASSIGNMENT:*
*Psalm 78:72; James 3:17*

## BE FAIR; REFRAIN FROM MAKING JUDGMENTS WITHOUT THE FACTS

The man who first discipled me as a new Christian and for whom I worked many summers at Bible camp always gave the same advice whenever we young people were involved in a conflict or debate: "Make no judgment without the facts." It's good advice for elders as well. The Bible says, "He who gives an answer before he hears, it is folly and shame to him" (Prov. 18:13). Those are serious words. Yet many church leaders jump to conclusions and speak before they have all the facts. So when making decisions and when dealing with rumors, accusations, or people problems, it is the elders' responsibility to get all the facts, both pro and con.

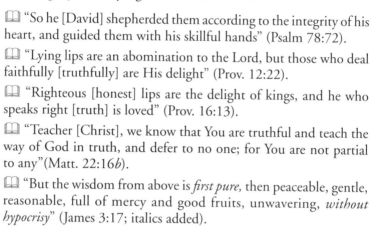

> **He who gives an answer before he hears, it is folly and shame to him. . . . The first to plead his case seems right, until another comes and examines him.** PROVERBS 18:13,17

It's natural to have an immediate reaction when we first hear of a problem or receive new information. But Scripture warns against hasty, one-sided judgments: "The first to plead his case seems right, until another comes and examines him" (Prov. 18:17). Thus elders must discipline themselves from making hasty judgments. They must do their homework and get the facts. Good information is essential to good decisions and sound judgments about people. Both sides of a case need to be heard before a judgment can be made.

**Elders must discipline themselves from making hasty judgments. They must do their homework and get the facts.**

Furthermore, it is essential to be open-minded and prepared to change. Determine to give others a fair, honest hearing. Scripture says that "the wisdom from above is ... reasonable [open to reason]" (James 3:17). It also says, "everyone must be quick to hear, slow to speak and slow to anger" (James 1:19). So seek by God's grace to be an objective listener and decision maker. After all, you would certainly want others to hear you with an open mind. Let the following verses remind you to listen carefully before making judgments:

- 🕮 "The way of a fool is right in his own eyes, but a wise man is he who listens to counsel" (Prov. 12:15).
- 🕮 "Through insolence [pride] comes nothing but strife, but wisdom is with those who receive counsel" (Prov. 13:10).
- 🕮 "The heart of the righteous ponders how to answer, but the mouth of the wicked pours out evil things" (Prov. 15:28).
- 🕮 "For the Lord is a God of justice" (Isa. 30:18*c*).
- 🕮 "Treat others the ... way you want them to treat you" (Luke 6:31).

*Scripture Memory Assignment:*
*Proverbs 18:13,17*

## Be Trustworthy with Confidential Information

An elder is in a position of trust. He is privy to private information about people, so he must understand the responsibility of confidentiality. To betray confidentiality can ruin an elder's reputation and discredit the entire leadership body. That is why the Scripture warns, "If you argue your case with a neighbor, do not betray another man's confidence, or he who hears it may shame you and you will never lose your bad reputation" (Prov. 25:9,10 NIV).

Private statements about other people in the church that are made by elders during a meeting must not be shared outside the meeting. In one case, an elder commented during the elders' meeting on the offensive behavior of one of the Sunday school teachers. Several days later, the elder received an angry phone call from that teacher. One of the other elders had repeated the conversation to the teacher without the elder council's permission. Such indiscretion destroys the elders' ability to talk to one another about private matters, and it destroys the congregation's trust in the elders.

To betray confidentiality can ruin an elder's reputation and discredit the entire leadership body.

To build trust with the congregation and among the elders, the elder council needs a policy of confidentiality. An elder must be trustworthy, and must not divulge confidential information: "He who goes about as a talebearer reveals secrets, but he who is trustworthy conceals a matter" (Prov. 11:13). A gossip, on the other hand, reveals secrets (Prov. 20:19). People will not share their secret sins and heartaches with their leaders if they can't trust them with private, personal information. Helping people with their problems demands protecting them from exposure to gossip. Furthermore, elders must be aware that in today's legal climate improperly divulging damaging information about a person can lead to a lawsuit.

An elder must think carefully before he shares information even with his spouse. There are issues an elder can discuss with his wife. There are issues on which he will receive good counsel from her. But there is also private information that should not be shared because it would be unfair to those who have confided in the elders. Moreover, exposing one's spouse to the sins of other people is potentially destructive to her relationships with them and to her spiritual life.

## Be Self-Controlled, Not Angry

Uncontrolled anger accentuates problems, clouds people's judgment, distorts reality, inflames emotions, deepens resentments, hinders peaceful problem solving, and provides the devil a prime opportunity to divide people (Eph. 4:26,27). So do not permit uncontrolled passions and anger to rule a meeting, no matter how controversial the topic of discussion may be. An out-of-control temper wounds the spirit and impedes the decision-making process. Uncontrolled anger is a primary reason that so many people are overcome by evil in their relationships with their Christian brothers and sisters (Rom. 12:21).

The Bible clearly and sternly warns against the widely destructive power of uncontrolled anger and says that a quick-tempered man cannot be an elder (Titus 1:7). An elder must be gentle, that is, forbearing and graciously amenable (1 Tim. 3:3). Moreover, the biblical qualifications for eldership stress the need for a leader in the church to be a person who is self-disciplined ("temperate," "prudent," "self-controlled"). So if ever an elder is out of control, yelling, making accusations and threats, or attacking another's character or motives, stop the meeting. Resume discussion only when the Spirit is once again in control.

**A gentle answer turns away wrath, but a harsh word stirs up anger.** PROVERBS 15:1

**Let your speech always be with grace, as though seasoned with salt, so that you will know how you should respond...** COLOSSIANS 4:6

Meditate on the following scriptural truths. Taking them to heart will make you a more self-controlled meeting participant.

- "There is one who speaks rashly like the thrusts of a sword, but the tongue of the wise brings healing" (Prov. 12:18).
- "A hot-tempered man stirs up strife" (Prov. 15:18*a*).
- "A fool always loses his temper" (Prov. 29:11*a*).
- "A hot-tempered man abounds in transgression" (Prov. 29:22*b*).
- "Be angry ... yet do not sin; do not let the sun go down on your anger, and do not give the devil an opportunity" (Eph. 4:26,27).
- "But now you also, put them all aside: anger, wrath, malice, slander, and abusive speech from your mouth" (Col. 3:8).
- "But everyone must be ... slow to anger; for the anger of man does not achieve the righteousness of God" (James 1:19*b*,20).

In sharp contrast to uncontrolled anger, wrath, bitterness, abusive speech, hot tempers, and cutting words, the Scripture encourages calmness, controlled anger, gentle talk, self-control, a cool and gracious spirit, healing words, and wise speech.

**Uncontrolled anger is a primary reason that so many people are overcome by evil in their relationships.**

Only by following scriptural principles of conduct can we hope to enjoy healthy group relationships and provide Christlike leadership for God's flock.

Take some time to read and consider the following passages. Allow them to sink deep into your heart and mind so that you can reflect more of God's character in your meetings.

- 🕮 "The tongue of the wise brings healing" (Prov. 12:18*b*).
- 🕮 "He who is slow to anger has great understanding" (Prov. 14:29*a*).
- 🕮 "A gentle answer turns away wrath, but a harsh word stirs up anger" (Prov. 15:1).
- 🕮 "A soothing tongue [speaking words that heal] is a tree of life" (Prov. 15:4).
- 🕮 "The slow to anger calms a dispute" (Prov. 15:18*b*).
- 🕮 "He who restrains his words has knowledge, and he who has a cool spirit is a man of understanding" (Prov. 17:27).
- 🕮 "Keeping away from strife is an honor for a man, but any fool will quarrel" (Prov. 20:3).
- 🕮 "A soft tongue breaks the bone" (Prov. 25:15*b*).
- 🕮 "Wise men turn away anger" (Prov. 29:8*b*).
- 🕮 "Let your speech always be with grace, as though seasoned with salt, so that you will know how you should respond to each person" (Col. 4:6).
- 🕮 "Who among you is wise and understanding? Let him show by his good behavior his deeds in the gentleness of wisdom" (James 3:13).

*Scripture Memory Assignment:*
*Proverbs 12:18; 15:1; 15:18; Colossians 4:6; James 1:19,20*

## PRINCIPLES OF EFFECTIVE COMMUNICATION

All elders' meetings involve people coming together to communicate with one another in order to accomplish their goal. Bruce Stabbert notes, "One of the most essential ingredients of any kind of teamwork is good communications."[2] Yet in many cases, atrocious communication exists among members of the eldership council and between the elders and the congregation.

Faulty communication has many detrimental effects:

- Poor group dynamics
- Inability to talk without getting into a fight
- Vague delegation of responsibilities, resulting in duplication and overlap
- Failure to respond to people's requests and questions
- Lack of follow-through on group tasks
- Confusion over the group's priorities
- Misunderstanding, suspicion, and isolation among various team members
- Hesitancy to direct or correct one another
- Failure to instruct or support people in fulfilling their responsibilities
- Difficulties in making decisions
- Poor morale among the elder team
- People routinely being hurt
- A frustrated, in-the-dark congregation

It's safe to say that anyone who is interested in sharing the gospel or shepherding God's flock should be concerned about improving his or her communication skills. Paul, for example, asked for prayer that he would communicate the gospel rightly and clearly, "in the way I ought to speak" (Col. 4:4). Church leadership also requires good verbal communication skills because they are essential to effective relationships, pastoral care, and productive meetings.

## Principles of Communication from Proverbs

God, in His divine wisdom, has given us everything we need pertaining to life and godliness (2 Peter 1:3). The Book of Proverbs has a great deal to say about speech and the power of words to heal or hurt, to unite or divide. From it we can identify some essential principles of good communication. These principles, consistently applied, will help us be effective communicators. Church leaders would do well to meditate on these verses and pray about areas that need improvement.

**Communication skills are essential to effective relationships, pastoral care, and productive meetings.**

**The wise seek to communicate well and for the blessing of others.**

📖 "A man will be satisfied with good [blessing; good things will result] by the fruit of his words" (Prov. 12:14*a*).

📖 "The tongue of the wise brings healing" (Prov. 12:18*b*).

📖 "A man has joy in an apt answer, and how delightful is a timely word!" (Prov. 15:23).

📖 "The words of a man's mouth are deep waters [profound]; the fountain of wisdom is a bubbling brook" (Prov. 18:4).

📖 "And sweetness of speech increases persuasiveness" (Prov. 16:21*b*).

📖 "Like apples of gold in settings of silver [signifying value, beauty, and skillfulness] is a word spoken in right circumstances" (Prov. 25:11).

**Good communication is controlled and guarded.**

📖 "When there are many words, transgression is unavoidable, but he who restrains his lips is wise" (Prov. 10:19).

📖 "The one who guards his mouth preserves his life" (Prov. 13:3*a*).

📖 "But he who repeats a matter separates intimate friends" (Prov. 17:9*b*).

📖 "A fool's lips bring strife" (Prov. 18:6*a*).

**Words can heal and encourage or hurt and destroy.**

📖 "There is one who speaks rashly like the thrusts of a sword [wound and kill], but the tongue of the wise brings healing" (Prov. 12:18).

📖 "Anxiety in a man's heart weighs it down, but a good [kind, encouraging] word makes it glad [cheers up]" (Prov. 12:25).

📖 "But a harsh word stirs up anger" (Prov. 15:1*b*).

📖 "Pleasant words are a honeycomb, sweet to the soul and healing to the bones" (Prov. 16:24).

📖 "Death and life are in the power of the tongue" (Prov. 18:21*a*).

**The best communication is always honest and truthful.**

📖 "Truthful lips will be established forever" (Prov. 12:19*a*).

📖 "Lying lips are an abomination to the Lord, but those who deal faithfully [truthfully] are His delight" (Prov. 12:22).

📖 "He who speaks right [truth] is loved" (Prov. 16:13*b*).

📖 "He kisses the lips [a sign of intimate, trusting friendship] who gives a right [honest, truthful] answer" (Prov. 24:26).

**The wise are good listeners, receptive to advice and correction.**

📖 "A wise man will hear" (Prov. 1:5*a*).

📖 "But a wise man is he who listens to counsel" (Prov. 12:15*b*).

📖 "The heart of the righteous ponders how to answer" (Prov. 15:28*a*).

📖 "A plan [or motive] in the heart of a man is like deep water, but a man of understanding draws it out [listens well and asks the right questions]" (Prov. 20:5).

📖 "Like an earring of gold and an ornament of fine gold is a wise reprover to a listening ear" (Prov. 25:12).

## Principles of Communication for Leaders

As a leader of people, be concerned about improving your ability to communicate. God is verbal and created us to be verbal creatures. We were made to communicate with God and people, but the Fall impaired this wondrous gift. Sin distorts our ability to communicate, creating many interpersonal problems. Poor communication causes unnecessary frustrations in a congregation. The guidelines listed below will improve your communication with your colleagues and with those you lead.

**Be aware that skillful communication is hard work.** Most people, especially men, are lazy communicators. They often don't care to expend the energy it takes to communicate well.

Make the effort to communicate better because you care for and love other people. "Better is open rebuke than love that is concealed" (Prov. 27:5). People desperately need to hear that they are loved, appreciated, and understood. As a leader, you are important to people in your congregation. They want to talk with you and hear from you. In all of Paul's letters, we see his exemplary ability to communicate with others on a meaningful level, to talk about difficult problems, to express his heartfelt love and sincere thankfulness, and to share his deep frustrations (see, for example, 2 Corinthians).

**Learn to speak gently, calmly, graciously, and tactfully.** This advice is solidly rooted in Scripture:

"A gentle answer turns away wrath, but a harsh word stirs up anger" (Prov. 15:1).

"Sweetness of speech increases persuasiveness" (Prov. 16:21*b*).

"By forbearance a ruler may be persuaded, and a soft tongue breaks the bone" (Prov. 25:15).

"Now I, Paul, myself urge you by the meekness and gentleness of Christ" (2 Cor. 10:1*a*).

"Let no unwholesome word proceed from your mouth, but only such a word as is good for edification according to the need of the moment, so that it will give grace to those who hear" (Eph. 4:29).

"Let your speech always be with grace [graciousness, attractiveness], as though seasoned with salt" (Col. 4:6*a*).

**Be aware of the ways you block good communication.** Lecturing and preaching, withdrawing or giving "the silent treatment," being easily angered or hurt, monopolizing conversations, being self-centered, avoiding real issues, and being argumentative or patronizing all destroy good communication, particularly with your loved ones and close friends. We all have communication weaknesses. Seek to be aware of the potential ways you block communication in your elders' meetings. With the Lord's help, work at improving your communication with your fellow colleagues.

**Make a conscious effort to be a patient listener.** "Effective leadership has more to do with listening than with talking."[3] While it is easier to talk than listen, being a good listener will enhance your pastoral care and improve your meeting participation. We could avoid tragic misjudgments and misunderstandings if only we would learn to listen better.

**People want to be heard and understood, but they often don't communicate clearly.**

People want to be heard and understood, but they often don't communicate clearly. So to be a good listener, don't assume you understand what other people are saying. Be patient, listen carefully, and don't be too quick to respond. Ask lots of questions to draw the speaker out. Work at understanding the other person's viewpoint and thought process. Make eye contact and notice body language. Listen for what is *not* said as well as what *is* said. If you make a habit of doing these things, you will reap the benefits of fewer misunderstandings and conflicts in your life and in your elders' meetings.

**Be proactive in your communication.** Because elders work under shared leadership, they must be able to talk to one another honestly and openly. If elders can't correct, challenge, and direct one another, they will be ineffective as a pastoral team.

**To be a good listener, don't assume you understand what other people are saying. Be patient, listen carefully, and don't be too quick to respond.**

The judgment of every elder is essential to sound group decision making, but the pressure to conform to the group's way of thinking or majority opinion can be so strong that sound, objective input is lost to the group. For the sake of preserving unity or personal friendships, some elders don't express their disagreement. Others may keep silent because they're afraid of appearing divisive. Still others avoid disagreeing with older, respected members. Such hesitation hurts group deliberations, hinders creativity, and stifles good decision making.

Every member of the elder council has a unique and important perspective. A healthy eldership team promotes an atmosphere that encourages everyone to speak up honestly without fear of rejection or attack. Elders must keep in mind the fact that the Spirit of God can use one dissenting voice to prevent the group from making a wrong decision. "Mature group members learn to disagree without being disagreeable, as the old line goes. They can express their opinions honestly, expecting that other colleagues will receive and consider them fairly."[4]

**If you have doubts . . . express them. Don't be silent! Have the courage to speak out.**

So an elder needs to express his thoughts honestly, without fear of being a dissenting voice. If you, for example, have doubts about a proposal or course of action, express them. Don't be silent! Have the courage to speak out. Your willingness to be forthright may prompt others to speak as well.

**Be sure to clarify responsibilities and work assignments.** Shared leadership requires continual communication among group members about their areas of responsibility and specific assignments. As the saying goes, "What is everyone's business is no one's business." If, for example, someone in the church is facing a life-or-death operation, what will happen if each elder thinks another is responsible to visit before the operation? It could be that not a single elder will visit because each one thinks someone else will be there. To avoid situations such as this, or to eliminate wasteful duplication of efforts, it is essential that elders clearly communicate their specific responsibilities, special assignments, and time commitments. This necessitates regular communication regarding ministry responsibilities.

**Provide adequate instruction when you give a person a job to do.** When giving someone a job to do, let that person know exactly what is expected. Don't assume that a person can read your mind or that he or she knows what the elder council wants. Let Jesus be your example. When He sent the Twelve out to preach, He told them in detail what to do, what to expect, and how to act (Matt. 10:1-11:1).

THAT'S NOT MY JOB

This is a story about four people named Everybody,
Somebody, Anybody, and Nobody.
There was an important job to be done and
Everybody was sure that Somebody would do it.
Anybody could have done it, but Nobody did it.
Somebody got angry about that,
because it was Everybody's job.
Everybody thought Anybody could do it,
but Nobody realized that Everybody wouldn't do it.
It ended up that Everybody blamed Somebody when
Nobody did what Anybody could have done.

**Don't leave people in the dark.** Let those you lead know your beliefs, vision, passion, and any changes in direction or policy. Communicate these matters regularly and clearly. Make your decisions known to all individuals and groups affected by them. Seek also to confer with key individuals or groups when making decisions. For example, the elders of one church announced to the congregation that the organ would no longer be used for church services. However, they neglected to discuss their decision with the four organists or the ten families that had bought the organ for the church. As a result, people left the church feeling angry and betrayed.

**Don't spring important decisions on people.** People want to participate in decisions that affect their ministry interests, so involve them in the decision-making process. Members of the congregation have wisdom, perspective, and information that may be extremely helpful in making sound decisions.

**Speak words of encouragement.** Let people know how they are doing in their respective ministries in the church. If they are doing a good job, tell them. People need to hear words of encouragement, and they need to hear them often. This is true within the elders' meetings as well. Be a Barnabas. Let people (including your fellow elders) know that you are thankful to God for them.

**Stop the rumor mill before it stops you.** Frequent, open communication with the congregation stops church rumors, so invite questions and keep open the lines of communication between the elders and the congregation. In times of trouble, communicate even more than you normally would. This is especially necessary in matters of church discipline or the exposure of public sin.

For example, a church was torn apart by a rumor that money had been embezzled by one of the elders and that the other elders were protecting the culprit. The rumor was untrue. But because the elders failed to quickly and forthrightly clarify the matter before the whole church, people were confused and lost trust in whatever the elders said.

## PRINCIPLES OF GOOD MEETING MANAGEMENT

Don't think for a moment that organization and management skills are unnecessary for the Spirit-indwelt family of God. The Bible says, "All things [even elders' meetings] must be done properly and in an orderly manner" (1 Cor. 14:40). The Holy Spirit specifically gifts people to lead

God's flock and manage God's household (Rom. 12:8; 1 Cor. 12:28; Eph. 4:11). Recognizing the need for leadership and management, the first Christian congregation under the apostles' leadership devised a strategy that would protect the apostles' ministry priorities and meet the needs of many poor widows (Acts 6:1-6). In contrast, the devil is the author of confusion, wasted time, and wasted gifts.

Management skills are important enough to the proper functioning of the eldership and the church family that the Holy Spirit requires a church elder to be able to manage his household well. The Spirit's logic says, in effect, that if a man can't manage properly his own household, he will not be able to manage properly the larger, extended household of the local church (1 Tim. 3:4,5).

The Bible also calls elders *God's stewards* (Titus 1:7). A "steward" (Greek, *oikonomos*) was often a slave who was entrusted with managing a household and was held accountable by the master of the household.

Furthermore, the Holy Spirit charges elders to *shepherd* God's flock. A shepherd is a manager or overseer. A shepherd of a literal flock of sheep must be skillful in land and water management so that he is able to provide water and grass for the sheep during the hot summer months. He must be able to treat sicknesses and watch for life-threatening diseases. He must protect the flock from predators and harsh weather. In a similar way, as Christ's undershepherds and God's stewards, elders have the responsibility and authority for the overall management and leadership of God's household. Good management is part of skillful stewardship and competent shepherding.

**Good management of God's household begins with good management of the elders' meetings.**

Good management of God's household begins with good management of the elders' meetings. A self-managed group such as a church eldership needs order, clear priorities, discipline, and self-evaluation or it becomes ineffective. The fact is, many elder councils tend to be unfocused, to grow accustomed to mediocrity, and to provide inadequate leadership. This is all the more reason for an elder council to conduct its meetings according to principles of sound group management and organization. Well-run meetings enhance leadership and build group morale. So consider some time-proven advice for improving the management of elders' meetings.

## Keep Priorities Straight

Church elders need desperately to understand their God-given priorities, or their meetings will be sidetracked quickly. There are qualified men who want to use their gifts to minister the Word or to shepherd people, but they will not participate in the eldership of their local churches because the elders' meetings are mired in the mud of administrative trivia. Many church elderships operate merely as glorified deacon boards or as building-maintenance committees. Sidetracked and distracted with details, they fail to lead the church.

One way to turn this problem around is to make meetings biblically focused. Redesign meetings and agendas to represent what the Bible says the role of the elders should be (see pp. 5-8). Then the elders will start functioning as a biblical eldership. Meetings will deal with truly important issues: defining and clarifying the church's beliefs and principles of ministry, developing a distinctive mission and vision, evaluating major ministries, improving pastoral care, and planning for the future.

The proper functioning of the eldership revolves around three core responsibilities: people, prayer, and the Word. These three things need to be constantly kept in focus when planning a meeting. Elders, of course, have other items of business to attend to, some of which are quite mundane, but these secondary items must not be allowed to dominate the elders' meetings, as is so often the case.

**There are qualified men who won't participate in the eldership of their local churches because the elders' meetings are mired in the mud of administrative trivia.**

## PEOPLE

The business of eldership is people business. The Holy Spirit calls the elders to pastor people (Acts 20:28; 1 Peter 5:1,2), and the Bible refers to the elders as the "elders of the people" (Ex. 19:7). Hebrews 13:17 beautifully describes their work as keeping "watch over your souls." James speaks of the elders' faith, prayers for, and counsel with the sick:

> Is anyone among you sick? Then he must call for the elders of the church and they are to pray over him, anointing him with oil in the name of the Lord; and the *prayer offered in faith* will restore the one who is sick,

and the Lord will raise him up, and *if he has committed sins,* they will be forgiven him." (James 5:14,15; italics added)

Additional passages emphasize the elders' responsibilities for people. Paul reminds the Ephesian elders, "you must help the weak" (Acts 20:35). The qualifications for Christian elders require them to be "hospitable" (1 Tim. 3:2) and able to teach people sound doctrine and protect them from false teaching (Titus 1:9). Elders are told to shepherd God's people (1 Peter 5:1,2), which means to lead, teach, protect, and practically care for people.

So elders must always be mindful that they lead God's precious family, God's congregation of redeemed people, God's household. The church is not a business organization, governmental agency, or military establishment; it is a household, a family. This focus on family and people requires a pastoral, fatherly orientation and style of leadership.

In order to fulfill their responsibilities to God's family, elders need to spend time talking about the needs of God's people. They need to inform one another about new people in the church as well as lost sheep who need to be pursued (an area of failure for most churches). They need to report on recent visits, urgent phone calls, and people who are ill. They need to support and advise one another when dealing with sinful people and difficult counseling situations. During their meetings elders need to assign and coordinate phone calls and visits that are necessary in fulfilling these responsibilities.

**The church is not a business organization, governmental agency, or military establishment; it is a household, a family.**

Elders need to invite key leaders of the church—the Sunday school superintendent, youth leaders, Bible study leaders, deacons, and committee leaders—to their meetings periodically for the purpose of exchanging information and maintaining accountability. The elders' caring direction and encouragement will help motivate these leaders to persevere and improve their ministries.

At times, others in the congregation may need to meet with the elders for special prayer, counsel, or discipline. Returning missionaries, for example, need private time with the elders to share special needs and to seek guidance. The elders, in turn, need to gather information from their missionaries so that they can pray intelligently, provide better assistance, encourage them effectively, and lead the congregation in financial and moral support.

Our Lord takes the elders' responsibilities to His people very seriously. Consider, for example, His strong words to Israel's shepherds:

> **Elders need to invite key leaders of the church to their meetings for the purpose of exchanging information and maintaining accountability. The elders' direction and encouragement will help motivate these leaders to persevere and improve their ministries.**

"Those who are sickly you have not strengthened, the diseased you have not healed, the broken you have not bound up, the scattered you have not brought back, nor have you sought for the lost; but with force and with severity you have dominated them" (Ezek. 34:4). The seriousness of the elders' responsibility for God's people is further emphasized by Scripture's command to the people of God's flock: "Obey your leaders and submit to them, for *they keep watch over your souls* as those who will give an account. Let them do this with joy and not with grief, for this would be unprofitable for you" (Heb. 13:17; italics added).

## PRAYER

The first church eldership body stated its priorities in magnificently succinct terms: "But we will devote ourselves to prayer and to the ministry of the word" (Acts 6:4). Prayer is not a formality for opening and closing a meeting; it is an essential part of the work, the special calling for all who lead God's people. Prayer should, therefore, be a significant part of all elders' meetings.

In every congregation, spiritual problems and physical needs exist for which the only solution is believing, persistent prayer. When confronted with a problem that His disciples could not resolve, our Lord said, "This kind cannot come out by anything but prayer" (Mark 9:29; cf. Matt. 17:20,21). In addition, the elders should devote themselves to the many private prayer needs that cannot be mentioned publicly.

Elders cannot be passive about prayer. Our Lord wasn't. Scripture plainly says that prayerlessness is disobedience and sin (1 Sam. 12:23; Luke 18:1). The following practical suggestions will help elders improve their prayer ministry, specifically during their meetings.

**Start with prayer.** In most cases, if elders wait until the end of the meeting, they will have little time and energy left for serious, earnest intercessory prayer on behalf of the flock. So it is best to start the elders' meetings with prayer. As soon as two people arrive, begin praying. If you start with prayer, you can always close the meeting with another short prayer time. The more prayer the better.

**Use a prayer guide.** I have visited elders' meetings in which twenty to thirty minutes was spent collecting prayer requests, which wastes valuable prayer time. A prepared, up-to-date prayer list allows elders to start praying for recognized needs immediately. Special requests can be interjected and written down at any time during prayer as requests come to mind. It takes conscientious effort to prepare a thorough, up-to-date prayer guide, so someone needs to dedicate time to this valuable task. (See Appendix B, p. 73, for a sample prayer guide).

**Appoint a prayer facilitator.** A prayer facilitator is responsible to keep the prayer time vital and productive. If he senses that prayer time is becoming sleepy time, he can introduce new prayer items or have the elders break into small prayer groups. There are many creative ways to energize a prayer meeting so that it doesn't become a dull routine. Whatever routine you use, change it occasionally.

**Pray shorter prayers.** Beware of long, drawn-out prayers. They can put even the most spiritually minded prayer warrior to sleep! Short, specific prayers, on the other hand, can help keep a group prayer meeting moving along. With short prayers, each elder can pray numerous times. Moreover, specific prayer items can be prayed for by several people. For instance, if a prayer item involves a person with cancer, one elder can pray for physical healing, another for the family, another for the financial needs, etc. This kind of praying puts life and energy into group prayer. Remember also to add your "Amens" to the prayers of others (1 Cor. 14:16). Let others know you're awake and in agreement with their prayers.

**It is important to actively and consistently seek prayer requests from the congregation.**

**Use prayer request cards.** Hudson Taylor, founder of the China Inland Mission (1865) and one of the great prayer warriors of all time, taught that information is key to keeping prayer vital.[5] The same is true for the local church. Firsthand, up-to-date information from the congregation energizes the elders' prayers and stirs their heart for the flock.

**Let people know that you are engaged in the ministry of prayer, that you labor passionately in prayer for them, and that you are men of faith and prayer.**

So it is important to actively and consistently seek prayer requests from the congregation. One way to do this is to make prayer request cards available so that people can write down their requests. Do all you can to let people know you are engaged in the ministry of prayer, that you labor passionately in prayer for them, and that you are men of faith and prayer (James 5:14,15).

**Break into small groups for prayer.** Divide the elders into groups of two for sharing personal needs and praying together for five or ten minutes. This helps members know each other better, minister to one another, and pray more. It will also enliven the prayer segment of the elders' meeting.

**Sing.** Singing together enhances prayer and praise. Singing together is a uniquely inspiring form of praise and prayer to God. Singing unites and focuses the group spiritually and expresses the Spirit's presence and control (Eph. 5:18,19).

**Be specific.** Pray for people by name. During the prayer time, choose several families to pray for. By doing this over a period of time, the elders will be able (in most cases) to pray together for each family in the congregation.

**Be creative, try new ideas, continually evaluate. Above all, pray!**

A vibrant prayer time prepares the elders for the rest of their meeting. This is especially true for those who have worked a long day before coming to a meeting. They may be tired and preoccupied with other matters. A dynamic prayer time can rejuvenate the spirit and refocus the mind for the work ahead.

If your prayer time is lifeless, address the problem immediately. Be creative, try new ideas, continually evaluate. Above all, pray! Let the following verses remind you of the importance and the privilege of prayer.

> 📖 "Moreover, as for me, far be it from me that I should sin against the Lord by ceasing to pray for you; but I will instruct you in the good and right way" (1 Sam. 12:23).
>
> 📖 "Now He was telling them a parable to show that at all times they ought to pray and not to lose heart" (Luke 18:1).
>
> 📖 "Epaphras … [is] always laboring earnestly for you in his prayers, that you may stand perfect and fully assured in all the will of God" (Col. 4:12).
>
> 📖 "The effective prayer of a righteous man can accomplish much" (James 5:16*b*).

## THE WORD OF GOD

Acts 6:4 is one of the most significant verses in the New Testament for church leaders: "But we will devote ourselves to prayer and to the ministry of the word." This statement, which "found approval with the whole congregation" (Acts 6:5*a*), established the fundamental priorities for church elders: prayer and the Word. Richard N. Longenecker, in *The Expositor's Bible Commentary,* says that the word *devote* "connotes a steadfast and single-minded fidelity to a certain course of action."[6] So pastor elders must steadfastly and single-mindedly give themselves to prayer and the Word.

**The elder council is responsible to oversee all of the teaching ministries of the church.**

As teachers and defenders of the Word, the elders need to be about the great business of the church's beliefs and mission. This means that a fundamental task of the elder council is to define, clarify, state, and continually restate the church's foundational, nonnegotiable beliefs, its unique doctrinal distinctives, its ministry priorities, its direction, its spiritual values, and its mission and vision (see Acts 15). When elders think and plan at this level, decisions and choices become simpler because they must be made in agreement with the previously stated beliefs, priorities, and mission.

In addition, the elder council is responsible to oversee all of the teaching ministries of the church—Sunday school, women's ministry, Bible studies, home-groups, evangelistic outreaches, and the preaching services. In practical terms, this means that the eldership needs to:

- Evaluate and plan its own teaching-feeding ministry
- Define and continually evaluate all major teaching-preaching services
- Assess Sunday school and Bible study material
- Assess and approve all those who teach in the church
- Provide doctrinal guidelines for all church teachers
- Set a tone for the way Scripture and doctrine are taught
- Plan for evangelism

**A fundamental task of the elder council is to define, clarify, state, and continually restate the church's foundational, nonnegotiable beliefs, its unique doctrinal distinctives, its ministry priorities, its direction, its spiritual values, and its particular mission and vision.**

Moreover, doctrinal questions will arise that require the elders to study and discuss Scripture together. Discussing doctrinal questions requires a good deal of time, yet it must be done because the local church is the "pillar and support of the truth" (1 Tim. 3:15).

Finally, the Word must be proclaimed to the world. We have a "great commission" (Matt. 28:18-20) and a big gospel. Elders need to think about, talk about, pray about, and plan for the spread of the Word, locally as well as globally, so that they can faithfully communicate a gospel-proclaiming vision to the church. Take time to meditate on the following verses and let the ministry of the Word have its rightful place in your heart.

📖 "Woe, shepherds of Israel who have been feeding themselves! Should not the shepherds feed the flock?" (Ezek. 34:2*b*).

📖 "My people are destroyed for lack of knowledge. Because you have rejected knowledge, I also will reject you from being My priest" (Hosea 4:6*a,b*).

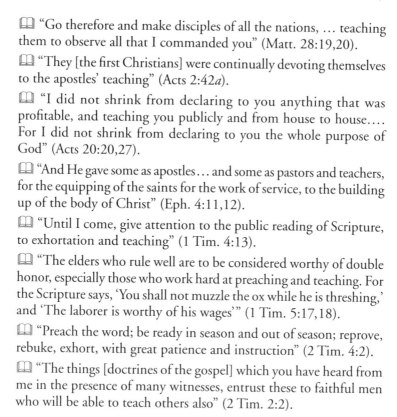

📖 "Go therefore and make disciples of all the nations, ... teaching them to observe all that I commanded you" (Matt. 28:19,20).

📖 "They [the first Christians] were continually devoting themselves to the apostles' teaching" (Acts 2:42*a*).

📖 "I did not shrink from declaring to you anything that was profitable, and teaching you publicly and from house to house.... For I did not shrink from declaring to you the whole purpose of God" (Acts 20:20,27).

📖 "And He gave some as apostles... and some as pastors and teachers, for the equipping of the saints for the work of service, to the building up of the body of Christ" (Eph. 4:11,12).

📖 "Until I come, give attention to the public reading of Scripture, to exhortation and teaching" (1 Tim. 4:13).

📖 "The elders who rule well are to be considered worthy of double honor, especially those who work hard at preaching and teaching. For the Scripture says, 'You shall not muzzle the ox while he is threshing,' and 'The laborer is worthy of his wages'" (1 Tim. 5:17,18).

📖 "Preach the word; be ready in season and out of season; reprove, rebuke, exhort, with great patience and instruction" (2 Tim. 4:2).

📖 "The things [doctrines of the gospel] which you have heard from me in the presence of many witnesses, entrust these to faithful men who will be able to teach others also" (2 Tim. 2:2).

*Scripture Memory Assignment:*
*Acts 6:4*

## Determine Frequency of Meetings

Building an effective pastoral eldership team requires frequent contact and time together that is not necessarily required of a board eldership. If a pastoral eldership team meets once a month for three hours, they will meet for thirty-six hours per year (assuming no cancellations). In the majority of cases, the real work of a pastoral eldership team cannot begin to be accomplished effectively in what amounts to less than one forty-hour workweek per year. So serious-minded pastor elders must make frequent meetings a priority.

The nature of pastoral work demands constant thought and attention to the needs of the flock. The natural tendency of any leadership group, however, is to lose momentum, energy, and effectiveness. To maintain forward momentum and to stay on top of problems and issues, frequent, regularly scheduled meetings are a necessity. Pastor elders need quality time to pray together, talk over doctrinal issues, discuss people concerns and missionary needs, engage in creative thinking and planning, and handle the practical matters they cannot delegate.

The elders' involvement in some issues will demand numerous, time-consuming meetings. A doctrinal issue, a case of church discipline, or a major policy change, for example, may require many hours of discussion conducted during a number of meetings. In addition, complex and utterly heartrending conflicts arise between people or families in the church. Such conflicts require careful thought and adequate time on the part of the elders to think through a course of action that will be fair to all parties. These kinds of conflicts cannot be rushed, nor can they be postponed, and they certainly cannot be handled adequately in a once-a-month meeting format. Too much time lapses between once-a-month meetings to allow for productive discussion and resolution of such difficult matters, and the decision-making process may drag on unduly.

**To maintain forward momentum and to stay on top of problems and issues, frequent, regularly scheduled meetings are a necessity.**

Frequent meetings help maintain close, regular contact between those elders who serve the church full time and those who do not. Those who do not serve full time can easily feel disconnected from the work. They may feel uninformed or even manipulated by those who have more time to think about and plan for the needs of the local church. If elders are not sensitive to this potential problem, there may be dissension, and the full-time elders may do all the work while the other elders are relegated to advisory status. When such a situation develops, there is little reason for all the elders to meet frequently. Indeed, it becomes an inconvenience to meet more than once a month. So frequent meetings are necessary to ensure healthy communication and full team cooperation.

Frequent meetings allow elders to keep up with their workload, and they also allow more time for fellowship and mutual support. When elders meet frequently enough to conduct their business in a timely manner, they can occasionally enjoy a relaxing dinner together in place of their regular meeting, which will strengthen their bond as Christian brothers. So the number of times a month your eldership meets should be given considerable thought.

The frequency of elders' meetings helps determine the duration of meetings. Frequent meetings generally mean shorter meetings. Elders who meet once a month normally engage in marathon meetings, which can be rushed, ineffective, and exhausting. Elders who meet only once a month may grow to dread their meetings.

> **Frequent meetings allow elders to keep up with their workload, and they also allow more time for fellowship and mutual support.**

Cancellation of meetings is another issue to consider. Some elders use any excuse to cancel a meeting: It's snowing, it's raining, it's too hot, too few men will be there. This is a mistake. Even if only two elders are available, they should meet and pray and do whatever business they can. They might use any time that is left for visitation. Canceling meetings quickly becomes a bad habit. Furthermore, it sends the wrong message: What we are doing isn't that important.

> **Canceling meetings quickly becomes a bad habit. It sends the wrong message: What we are doing isn't that important.**

## Start on Time, End on Time

For some groups, starting late, being unprepared, wasting time, ignoring or neglecting duties, procrastinating, and canceling meetings is standard practice. Although it may be standard practice, such behavior shows disrespect for the King of kings, the Lord Jesus Christ, and His precious flock. It is spiritual laziness—giving God the crumbs of least effort rather than the best fruit of time and energy (Rom. 12:11).

Starting late establishes poor group discipline. It punishes those who are on time and reinforces the latecomer's behavior. It communicates that being late doesn't matter; that nothing important happens at these meetings; thus they don't need to be taken seriously. So begin meetings promptly at the appointed time. If even two people are present, one of them needs to take charge and start praying.

It is also important to schedule an ending time and seek to end at that time. Of course there are occasions when it is necessary and productive to extend the meeting time to finish an important discussion, but this should be the exception, not the rule. If a meeting must go substantially overtime, poll the group members for their agreement and renegotiate

> **Begin meetings promptly at the appointed time. If even two people are present, one of them needs to take charge and start praying.**

the ending time. This shows respect for their schedules. Protracted meetings wear people down. When they are tired and want to go home, people tend to make hasty decisions simply to end a meeting.

## Establish a Conducive Meeting Place

Where you meet does affect your meetings. I once attended an elders' meeting in a damp, poorly lit church basement. We sat for several hours on hard benches with no back support. It was a depressing, uncomfortable atmosphere. It made me want to get out of the meeting as quickly as possible and not return.

Adequate lighting, comfortable chairs, plenty of table space, good ventilation, pleasant room temperature, and adequate privacy all help to energize a meeting and make it more productive. Having drinks and light snacks available at your meetings is also appreciated. Refreshments help elders stay alert and focused.

If you meet in a home, ensure that others living in the home cannot overhear your discussion. And don't be within earshot of a telephone; you don't want your meeting to be interrupted by its ringing.

Out of respect for your colleagues and the significance of your limited time together, turn off pagers and cell phones unless keeping them on is absolutely necessary. In order to protect customers from annoying phone ringing and loud talking, some restaurants now request that their guests refrain from using cell phones in the dining room.[7] It's good advice for meetings and it's just good cell phone etiquette.

> **Turn off pagers and cell phones unless keeping them on is absolutely necessary.**

Try also to avoid being called out of a meeting for non-emergency reasons. Inform family and friends of your need for uninterrupted time with your pastoral colleagues. Set a time for people to call you after the meeting if they need to talk to you.

## Develop an Agenda

A major cause of frustration with elders' meetings is the fact that no one takes responsibility to prepare for their success. Many elders would agree with the saying that "a committee keeps minutes but wastes hours." Meetings, however, do not have to be time killers. They can be productive and fulfilling when prayer and thoughtful preparation are given beforehand.

> **Someone needs to expend the time and effort necessary to prepare the group's agenda.**

One critical element of an effective meeting is a prepared agenda. "An agenda is crucial to a meeting's success. It puts the meeting's purpose in focus and sets the tone for the task at hand. It is also the best tool for controlling the meeting's progress."[8] Experience has shown that adequate time spent in preparing an agenda, talking it over with others, thinking it through carefully, prioritizing items, and eliminating needless items guarantees a more productive meeting. This point can hardly be overemphasized. Someone (or more than one) needs to expend the time and effort necessary to prepare the group's agenda.

Some elders are concerned that preparing an agenda eliminates—or even hinders—the work of the Holy Spirit. Nothing could be further from the truth. A planned agenda no more eliminates the Spirit's work than a planned sermon eliminates His work. The Holy Spirit works in both the thoughtful planning of an agenda and its implementation. An agenda is simply a tool that helps manage the elders' workload during their brief time together. It provides order, purpose, and focus. It helps the elders budget their time and separate trivial items of business that need only minutes of discussion from weighty items that require hours of concentrated deliberation. An agenda protects the group from exasperating bunny trails into side issues and keeps them focused on the subject at hand. It sets limits on potential marathon discussions and screens out items that should be delegated to the deacons, other committees, or individuals in the church.

Whether it is simple or elaborate, an agenda should serve the elders' priorities. Evaluating and improving an agenda so that it continues to facilitate effective meetings is an ongoing process. Consider the following guidelines and suggestions for developing a helpful agenda. (A sample agenda is provided in Appendix C, p. 75.)

> Adequate time spent in preparing an agenda, talking it over with others, thinking it through carefully, prioritizing items, and eliminating needless items guarantees a more productive meeting.

**Make the agenda open to all.** All elders are free to place items on the agenda by contacting in advance (by phone, e-mail, or fax) the person responsible for preparing the agenda.

**Give advance notice.** If possible, send a tentative agenda to all participants a few days before a meeting.

**Don't overload the agenda.** Plan for what can be reasonably accomplished in the time available. Don't try to put four hours of content into a two-hour time frame. Don't try to force a heavy discussion item into the last few minutes of a meeting.

**Identify the need for special meetings or subcommittees.** If the agenda becomes backlogged with issues that require hours of discussion, it may occasionally be necessary to schedule a separate meeting or to appoint a subcommittee of elders to handle specific tasks. When an eldership cannot accomplish all of its work during the regular meeting time, a subcommittee of elders may be appointed to do outside work. A subcommittee might develop policies, programs, and solutions or prepare doctrinal studies for the eldership to discuss and act on at a later date.

For example, the elders may want to write or revise the church's vision statement, in which case they spend several hours discussing their thoughts. Then a subcommittee of elders takes the ideas generated by the whole eldership and begins to work out the details and write a proposed vision statement. Later, their work is presented to the eldership team for correction, refinement, and final approval.

**Identify structured and nonstructured discussion items.** A special agenda can be made for guiding major discussions, especially hard-to-manage and often lengthy doctrinal discussions. A good agenda and orderly facilitation help complex discussions move along more smoothly. Sometimes, however, a group needs unstructured, free-flowing discussion time. A good agenda (and facilitator) will distinguish between structured discussions and free-flowing time segments and will designate these times appropriately.

**Create an agenda for outside participants.** At times, other church leaders will need to meet with the eldership (see pp. 43, 44). When key ministry leaders meet to consult with the elders, it is usually best to help them prepare an agenda for their discussion. Otherwise, participants may talk aimlessly and accomplish little. There are, of course, times when the purpose of the meeting is to have a free and open discussion.

**Plan future topics of discussion.** Several times a year the elders should discuss what major topics need to be placed on future agendas. These items should include important church issues and ministries that require periodic discussion such as prayer ministry, Bible-teaching ministry, local evangelism, world outreach, future direction, or leadership training. Such items, although important, may otherwise never be talked about because of the relentless demands of the moment.

By planning future items for discussion, the elders take control of the content of their agenda, ensuring that topics crucial to the spiritual health of the church are not ignored. The eldership thus becomes proactive, rather than reactive, in its leadership. Sadly, many elderships are always two or three steps behind everything. They have a maintenance mentality rather than a leadership mentality. Placing items for future discussion on an agenda helps the elders think about the larger picture and the long-range shepherding needs of the flock. It also helps them move out of the maintenance mode into the leadership mode of pastoral oversight.

**End conclusively.** Meetings can become substitutes for taking action, so it is important for an agenda to include time for summary conclusions and assignments. Proverbs reminds us, "In all labor there is profit, but mere talk leads only to poverty" (Prov. 14:23).[9] Don't let a meeting fizzle out like a car out of gas on a busy highway. At the end of the meeting, summarize what has been decided and accomplished. Restate all assignments and who is responsible for the completion of each. "Most decisions are not an end; rather, they are part of a process of getting something done. ... Decisions require action: Somebody must do something as a result."[10]

Making a decision and implementing it are two different things. The Christians at Corinth, for example, had decided to give money to their poor brethren in Jerusalem. Although they were willing to give, they didn't follow through. Paul had to remind them, "Now finish doing it also, so that just as there was the readiness to desire it, so there may be also the completion of it by your ability" (2 Cor. 8:11).

**By planning future items for discussion, the elders take control of the content of their agenda, ensuring that topics crucial to the spiritual health of the church are not ignored. The eldership thus becomes proactive, rather than reactive, in its leadership.**

Christians today still fail to follow through, and the consequences can be hurtful. The elders of one church, for example, decided to dismiss the Sunday school superintendent because of his poor church attendance and critical spirit. They forgot to assign someone to tell the superintendent of their decision, however; he learned of his dismissal during a prayer meeting. He and his family were hurt and angered by the elders' insensitive handling of the situation.

**At the end of the meeting, summarize what has been decided and accomplished. Restate all assignments and who is responsible for the completion of each.**

Obviously such oversights are to be avoided. After a decision is made, specific action steps need to be outlined. The three key questions that always need to be answered are:

- What specifically needs to be done?
- Who is responsible to carry out the decision?
- When will it be done?

## Identify the Role of the Facilitator

The role of the facilitator is crucial to productive meetings. The verb *facilitate* means "assist" or "expedite." It also conveys the idea of making something easier. The facilitator serves as a contact person for the group and schedules visitors. The facilitator helps the group function more efficiently and makes group interaction easier. Hence, he must have "an unwavering dedication to serving the needs of the group."[11] To be truly effective, a facilitator needs to do several things.

**Think ahead.** The facilitator guides the group through its planned agenda. To do this, he must think ahead, not so much about the content as about the process. What kind of meeting will it be? A problem-solving meeting, a decision-making meeting, a brainstorming meeting, a planning meeting, or a combination of the above? What information should be provided and which people need to be present for the meeting to run smoothly? Is it likely to be difficult and protracted? Can the facilitator do anything to reduce the stress levels of those attending? Will the facilitator need to be firm and directive, or will he be able to be more relaxed in his leadership style?

**Guide and guard the discussion.** A good facilitator impartially guides the discussion and decision-making process, ensuring that each member participates freely and is treated fairly. He enhances active group participation and protects the group from being dominated by any one person. He skillfully handles "over-talkers," who, observe Roger Mosvick and Robert Nelson in their *Guide to Successful Meeting Management*, "say more than they need to, repeat themselves unnecessarily, and speak when they have nothing substantive to add to the discussion."[12]

An aggravating but common problem that can be particularly trying to any facilitator is dealing with members who derail the agenda or discussions with side issues. A good way to handle the introduction of side issues is to have a "Future Discussion Items" list at the bottom of the agenda. When someone brings up an issue that is off the subject and outside the agenda, the facilitator simply suggests that it be placed on

**A good facilitator enhances active group participation and protects the group from being dominated by any one person.**

the list and then returns to the discussion at hand. Those who tend to derail meetings with stories or items of personal interest should be treated kindly but firmly. It is the responsibility of the facilitator to protect the group from excessive interruptions and from five-minute discussions turning into forty-five-minute ones.

**Balance control with flexibility.** Conversely, the facilitator must not over-control or micromanage the discussion process. Over-control stifles group interaction and creativity. A heavy-handed facilitator crushes healthy spontaneity and interaction among group members. A good facilitator recognizes the group's need for both flexibility and control.

**Move forward and summarize clearly.** The facilitator sensitively nudges the group toward concluding and clarifying decisions. Inconclusive discussions and decisions are common frustrations. The group jumps to the next topic before completing the first one—before it has been brought to proper closure. Decisions are vague and poorly articulated. People leave the meeting unsure of what has been decided.

To avoid such frustrations, the facilitator should clearly summarize what has been decided so that everyone understands the decision that has been made, and knows what needs to be done and by whom. Any member of the group should feel comfortable saying, "I am unclear about what has been decided," or "Wait a minute; we're not ready to move to the next topic. I'm not in agreement with the present summary of our decision."

> Inconclusive discussions and decisions are common frustrations. The group jumps to the next topic before completing the first one. Decisions are vague and poorly articulated. People leave the meeting unsure of what has been decided.

**Follow through.** The facilitator (or someone he appoints) ensures that decisions are implemented. He makes sure things get done. He reminds fellow members of their assigned tasks.

**Evaluate effectiveness.** A good facilitator regularly seeks to evaluate the effectiveness of the meetings, always looking for ways to improve procedures and dynamics. Each meeting can be a learning experience that results in better future meetings.

A facilitator takes charge of the process of a meeting, but he is by no means the sole speaker. In fact, a facilitator usually remains neutral on issues so he can facilitate the group's discussion objectively and fairly. When he wishes to present his opinions, he may hand over facilitation of the meeting to another elder. In a small eldership this may be impractical, but in a larger group a leader may sometimes choose not to facilitate major discussions in order to be free to concentrate on the content rather than the process of a discussion.

It's important to note that having a facilitator does not exclude other members from exercising leadership in the meeting or from active participation. All elders should lead at different times and in different ways. Also, the eldership of a large church with several staff members will operate differently than a two-man eldership of a house church. The following practical suggestions, adapted to your particular situation, can greatly improve group facilitation.

**Take a team approach**. Use several facilitators during the course of a meeting. For example, one elder facilitates the group's prayer time, another facilitates the quick business items segment, a different elder facilitates the major discussion (the most difficult part), and another provides a summary of the meeting's decisions, accomplishments, and assigned tasks. This approach works especially well for elders' meetings because they tend to be long and involved.

**Meetings are energized when a number of participants are involved in the process of facilitation because more people are assuming responsibility for their success.**

It's important for a person to facilitate the part of the meeting that he is most capable of facilitating. If the elder facilitating the major discussion time cannot keep discussions on track, is not time-sensitive, is afraid to correct problem members, can't follow complex discussions, can't handle details, or can't nudge members to make a decision, the elders will become frustrated. If an elder doesn't feel capable of facilitating a long, complex discussion, he shouldn't feel pressured to do so. He can facilitate another segment of the meeting.

In addition to the facilitator(s), other elders are also involved in managing a meeting. The group needs a recorder (secretary) to take minutes because a facilitator cannot both record minutes and keep his mind on guiding the discussion. Some groups also use a timekeeper. Meetings are energized when a number of participants are involved in the process because more people are assuming responsibility for their success.

**Rotate facilitation.** Try rotating facilitation among various members of the eldership team. When people learn the skills and experience the frustrations of facilitation, they become better group participants. A person who has facilitated a meeting has a greater awareness of what good group participation means and can be a better participant. In addition, if one facilitator is absent, another can easily fill in. If, however, a person has proven to be an excellent facilitator, the group may decide to keep him in that role indefinitely.

## Keep Minutes and Records

Since the elders' decisions represent and affect the whole congregation, they must be recorded. Some government agencies require churches to keep written records for tax status or benefits. Church discipline cases especially need to be documented in order to help protect the congregation from legal action. (Churches named in lawsuits have had their elders' minutes subpoenaed.)

Minutes should include the meeting date, names of persons present, key points of discussion, decisions, and follow-up activities including the names of those who are responsible for assignments. Minutes need not be elaborate, except in matters such as church discipline, doctrinal changes, or major policy decisions.

Minutes should be made available to the eldership team within several days of a meeting. Some groups e-mail their minutes for correction and approval so that changes can be made prior to the next meeting. This provides each participant an opportunity to carefully review the minutes beforehand and thus allows for them to be read with fewer interruptions at the next meeting.

Reading the minutes at the beginning of a meeting provides a regular, formal means of checking on the previous meeting's assignments. It calls each elder to accountability. If the minutes are long and detailed, then only the highlights, summaries, and assignments of the previous meeting should be read and approved.

In addition to the minutes, written records also need to be kept of the many policy decisions an elder council makes. Over time, it's easy to forget the exact details of these decisions. Establishing policies for the congregation is an essential part of good governing; it is also time-consuming, hard work. But it is a very necessary, practical way that the elder council consistently governs and communicates decisions.

**Written records need to be kept of the many policy decisions an elder council makes.**

Policies are needed for a variety of matters such as building use, weddings, music ministry, financial management, missions, etc. But policies are worthless if they cannot be found or if they are out of date. Written records of these policies (or any major decisions) should not be scattered throughout years of elders' meeting minutes only, but a detailed record of these policies should also be kept in a special policy notebook. This notebook should be brought to every elders' meeting so that the elders have easy access to any policy or major decision. Remember to date all official papers and letters and include the names of all persons involved in making the decision or in establishing a policy.

Furthermore, new members need immediate orientation to the elder council's policies, major decisions, beliefs, and procedures if they are to participate intelligently. They can't do this if there are no available records. It also would be helpful to a new elder to know the eldership's historical beginnings, major changes and events, key decisions, doctrinal shifts, and notable personages. A brief, written history of your eldership would give a new member an immediate sense of continuity that otherwise could take years to develop.

**New members need immediate orientation to the elder council's policies, major decisions, beliefs, and procedures if they are to participate intelligently. They can't do this if there are no available records.**

## Delegate, Delegate, Delegate

Elders need to remember they are not the sole ministers of the congregation. They cannot and should not be doing everything in the church, but in many churches they do. In one case, a group of elders spent more than an hour deciding which carpet cleaning company to use. Instead, they should have spent thirty seconds delegating the work to others.

Better yet, they should have established a committee to be responsible for cleaning and maintaining the building so that they could focus on leading God's people.

The Lord's people comprise a royal priesthood and a Spirit-indwelt body in which each member is responsible to minister to one another. Thus the work of the local church is to be shared by all its members. If elders teach, organize, encourage, and empower the people properly, many within the congregation should be involved in ministering to one another and reaching out to nonbelievers. Consider the following verses that describe the gifts and work of the church body:

> "For just as we have many members in one body [the physical body] and all the members [parts of the body] do not have the same function, so we, who are many, are one body in Christ, and individually members one of another. Since we have gifts that differ according to the grace given to us, each of us is to exercise them accordingly" (Rom. 12:4-6*a*).
>
> "Now there are varieties of gifts, but the same Spirit. And there are varieties of ministries, and the same Lord.... But to each one is given the manifestation of the Spirit for the common good.... For the body is not one member, but many.... But now God has placed the members, each one of them, in the body, just as He desired" (1 Cor. 12:4,5,7,14,18).
>
> "But to each one of us grace was given according to the measure of Christ's gift" (Eph. 4:7).
>
> "As each one has received a special gift, employ it in serving one another as good stewards of the manifold grace of God" (1 Peter 4:10).

The elders prod, equip, protect, mobilize, approve, and lead, but all of God's people are called to serve (Eph. 4:11,12). So the elders should not do everything, nor should they allow people to assume that they do. Elders need to avail themselves of all the resources of the congregation and spread out the work of the church. The message elders ought to send to the people is the same as this message of Paul to the Christians at Corinth:

> Therefore, my beloved brethren, be steadfast, immovable, *always abounding in the work of the Lord, knowing that your toil is not in vain in the Lord.* (1 Cor. 15:58; italics added)

As a leadership council, the elders put structures in place so that many people can serve together in an organized, approved, orderly manner. Elders should delegate as much as possible to others. So they shouldn't put items on their agenda that can easily be delegated. In order to delegate well, elders can learn from Acts 6:1-6 some key principles of delegation:

- Identify what needs to be done.
- Select the right people.
- Tell people what is expected of them.
- Give people the proper authority, accountability, and ownership to make the job fulfilling.
- Let people know that they are appreciated and that the elders are there to help.

## Practice Self-Evaluation

Like any other leadership body, a church eldership can always improve. No one knows it all. No one has graduated from Christ's school of learning. We all have much yet to learn (and unlearn).

Good meetings can get better, and good leaders can become better leaders. In order to improve their meetings and their pastoral

> **It is important to create an atmosphere in which self-evaluation is welcomed, expected, and a normal part of the elders' work.**

leadership, it is important for elders to create an atmosphere in which self-evaluation is welcomed, expected, and a normal part of their work. Self-satisfaction is a deception that stunts improvement, growth, and learning. It is also contrary to Scripture: "A wise man will hear and increase in learning" (Prov. 1:5*a*).

Self-evaluation is essential for the improvement of a self-managed group of elders. It's easy to fall into a rut, to do little when in fact there is much to do, to stop learning when there is much yet to learn, and to stop growing when much growth remains. So elders should periodically evaluate and rethink the effectiveness and organization of their meetings. They should seek to learn from their mistakes and make each meeting count for the glory of God. As Scripture says, "Take pains with these things; be absorbed in them [total commitment], so that *your progress* [advancement] *will be evident* [visible] *to all"* (1 Tim. 4:15; italics added). Few things are as thrilling to a congregation as watching its spiritual leaders grow, learn, and move forward with fresh ideas and vision.

It's also a good practice for the elders to evaluate every major church social activity, teaching series, baptismal service, or outreach event while the details are still fresh. They should write down their observations and proposed changes in order to continually improve the church's programs and activities. Evaluations should be kept in a file that can be referred to the next time the same event is planned.

Self-evaluation is essential for the improvement of a self-managed group of elders.

I can think of no better way to close than with Paul's exhortation to the first Christians in Rome. Like the early Christians, we, too, need constant encouragement to take action and be zealous for our Lord. So let these God-breathed words from Romans 12:11 inspire you to action and save your church from lukewarm, half-hearted Christianity.

**Not lagging behind in diligence:** "Paul is telling the Romans that where zeal is needed, they must not be lazy people."[13]

**Fervent in spirit:** "It is important that the human spirit be on fire, but Paul is not referring to something that occurs by some natural process but as a result of the indwelling Spirit of God."[14]

**Serving the Lord:** "The verb points to thoroughgoing devotion, service like of a slave."[15]

So as we seek to improve the effectiveness of our pastoral leadership meetings, let us act with diligence in service to our Lord—the Chief Shepherd, Jesus Christ.

*Scripture Memory Assignment:*

*Proverbs 1:5; Romans 12:11*

*Part Three*

# Questions and Assignments

**BEFORE BEGINNING THE QUESTIONS** and assignments, read the entire book. Some of the issues addressed in the questions and assignments touch sensitive areas. So be honest with one another, but understanding. Old habits are hard to break, and most people don't like to change. Look for creative alternatives to solve disagreements over some of these issues. Think and pray!

The questions and assignments are divided into four group sessions. For some groups, one question may take an entire session to discuss and plan how to implement. Take the time needed to complete all the assignments and questions.

**Session One**

1. List what the New Testament defines as duties of the church elders. Include biblical references with each statement. (See pp. 5-8, 40-43.)

2. Explain what is meant by "equality and diversity" within the eldership. (See Appendix A, p. 69.)

3. Discuss the importance of what you consider to be the three top reasons for having regular elders' meetings.

4. Have each person write down the three aspects of your meetings that are most frustrating and need improvement. Rank them from 1 to 3 in the order of most frustrating to least frustrating. Next, list the two most enjoyable aspects of your meetings. Appoint someone to record and categorize all the responses. For example, "Four out of five listed lack of prayer as their number one frustration with the meetings." This assignment will help the group identify

strengths and weaknesses of your meetings. As you continue through these sessions, you will begin making a plan for improvements.

5. People often want to know where to start when trying to improve their meetings. The best starting point is with the prayer time, even if it is only a five- or ten-minute segment of your meeting. Use the prayer suggestions on pages 45-47 to launch a discussion of various ways your prayer time together could be improved. Decide which ones you would like to try, and then discuss when and how you will implement these suggestions or your own ideas.

**Session Two**

1. Discuss how to improve the physical atmosphere of your meeting place (p. 52). What changes would you like to see made? Which are most important?

2. Read and discuss together ideas on facilitation (pp. 57-60) that you could implement to improve the quality of your meetings.

3. Start preparing guidelines and a list of helpful tips for your facilitators. Use the material in this book for a start. Both the guidelines and the list of tips for facilitators can be added to and improved upon over time.

4. Discuss the importance of starting on time and ending on time.

5. Discuss the number of times per month you should meet.

**Session Three**

1. Read and discuss as a group each of the agenda ideas listed on pages 54-57. Which ones do you need to implement to improve the quality of your meetings?

2. As a group, do you understand what is meant by taking responsibility for the content of your agenda (see p. 55)? Discuss your understanding of this important point as well as what improvements you think need to be made.

3. Discuss how to save time for more important matters by eliminating trivial or unnecessary business. At the same time, discuss what work or tasks you can delegate to others in the church.

4. List ways you can improve your record keeping.

5. If your group is interested in having more effective meetings, discuss how to begin making needed changes and implementing the suggestions in this book. Who will take responsibility for prodding the group to make improvements? What guidelines or timelines should the group provide the person(s) appointed to facilitate?

**Session Four**

1. Identify where you are weakest in communication among yourselves and with the congregation. What can you do to improve communication between members of the elder council and between the elders and the congregation?

2. As a group, do you understand what is meant by the following statements (from p. 47). Have several members explain these statements, and encourage others to add their comments:

   A fundamental task of the elder council is to define, clarify, state, and continually restate the church's foundational, nonnegotiable beliefs, its unique doctrinal distinctives, its ministry priorities, its direction, its spiritual values, and its mission and vision (see Acts 15). When elders think and plan at this level, decisions and choices become simpler because they must be made in agreement with the previously stated beliefs, priorities, and mission.

3. In which areas of defining and clarifying beliefs and mission or vision are you as an elder council deficient?

4. In what specific ways are you teaching and modeling your beliefs, special doctrinal distinctives, and particular mission or vision?

5. Schedule a meeting or two to discuss the entire teaching-feeding ministry of your local church. Brainstorm every aspect of your church's teaching ministry, listing both strengths and weaknesses. For example:
   - Are the children memorizing Scripture?
   - Are there doctrines and portions of the Bible your children or teens are not being taught?
   - Do you have classes to teach the fundamentals of the faith to new believers or new attendees?
   - Do you, like Paul, teach the full plan and counsel of God (Acts 20:27)?
   - What are you trying to accomplish through the Sunday morning sermons?
   - Do you know what the Sunday school teachers and youth leaders of your church believe?
   - Who checks and approves teachers in your church?

*Appendix A*

# Equality and Diversity within the Eldership

**IN WORDS DIRECTED TO THE ELDERS** of the church at Ephesus Paul said, "The Holy Spirit has made you [all of you] overseers, to shepherd the church of God" (Acts 20:28). He later wrote to the church at Ephesus, "The elders who rule well [some elders] are to be considered worthy of double honor, especially those who work hard at preaching and teaching" (1 Tim. 5:17). From these two magisterial, pivotal texts addressed to the church at Ephesus, we learn that both equality and diversity exist within a biblical eldership.

On the side of equality (also called parity of the eldership) the Scripture teaches that all the elders:

- Have been placed in the flock by the Holy Spirit as "overseers" for the specific purpose "to shepherd the church of God" (Acts 20:28)
- Have been charged by the Holy Spirit to "shepherd [pastor] the church of God" (Acts 20:28; 1 Peter 5:1,2)
- Share equally the authority and responsibility for the pastoral oversight of the entire congregation: "Be on guard ... for *all the flock*" (Acts 20:28; italics added)
- Are equally responsible to be alert to the constant dangers of false teaching and to guard the flock from false teachers (Acts 15:6; 20:28-31; Titus 1:9-13)
- Are to be able to teach Scripture and rebuke false teachers (1Tim. 3:2; Titus 1:9)
- Are to be publicly examined as to the biblical qualifications before serving as an overseer (1 Tim. 3:10; 5:22-25)
- Are responsible to visit and pray for the sick (James 5:14)
- Share the designations "elder" and "overseer" (Phil. 1:1; 1 Tim. 5:17)

- Are equally accountable to the entire eldership body and under the loving pastoral care of the entire eldership body (Acts 20:28*a*)
- Are to be appreciated, esteemed "very highly in love," honored, protected from slander, and obeyed (1 Thess. 5:12,13; 1 Tim. 5:17,19; Heb. 13:17)

Although all elders share equally the same office and pastoral charge, there is at the same time rich diversity of giftedness and life situations among those within the eldership. It is obvious that not all elders on an elder council are equal in giftedness, effectiveness, influence, time availability, experience, verbal skills, leadership ability, or biblical knowledge. Note the following scriptural references to diversity within the eldership:

- Not all elders labor diligently "at preaching and teaching" (1 Tim. 5:17). Although all elders must be able to teach, to refute false teachers, and be spiritually alert to the dangers of false doctrine, not all have the spiritual gift of teaching or evangelism or the same degree of proficiency at teaching or preaching the gospel. This implies that some elders (or one elder) will have a more prominent role in the public teaching ministry to the whole church.
- Not all elders "rule well [a marked proficiency]" (1 Tim. 5:17). Although all elders must be able to lead and manage their homes well, not all have the spiritual gift of leadership or the same degree of leadership skills (Rom. 12:8). This implies that one or some elders will display more prominent leadership initiative and influence within the eldership body.
- Not all elders receive financial compensation or the same amount of compensation (1 Tim. 5:18; Gal. 6:6).
- Not all elders receive "double honor" from the congregation and its elders, but it is mandated that the elders laboring in the Word be compensated for their diligent labor (1 Tim. 5:17,18). This implies that the elders and congregation acknowledge, set aside, and support those elders who labor in the gospel and equip the saints by the Word (Eph. 4:11). So Scripture supports both equality and diversity within a church eldership council.

The New Testament beautifully illustrates the concept of equality and diversity within the eldership by means of the twelve apostles. Our Lord appointed twelve apostles, not one apostle with eleven advisers. He trained and sent out all twelve to preach and heal (Matt. 10:1–11:1). He never trained any man alone, nor did He appoint one man head of His Church. He dedicated Himself to training a team of men who would eventually work together as a leadership body.

Yet within the apostolic team, Peter, James, and John stand out among their colleagues as exceptional leaders. Peter especially stands out as the chief speaker of the apostolic body and the prominent figure among the Twelve—the first among equals (Matt. 10:2; Luke 22:32).[1] Yet despite his prominence, Peter is considered *one* of the pillars of the church, not *the* pillar (Gal. 2:9).

First Timothy 5:17,18 is the key text that acknowledges diversity within the eldership council. Paul tells Timothy and the congregation that "the elders who rule well are to be considered worthy of double honor, especially those who work hard at preaching and teaching. For the Scripture says, 'You shall not muzzle the ox while he is threshing,' and 'The laborer is worthy of his wages.'"

**Certain elders, not all elders, are to receive double honor.**

Elders who lead "well" and especially those who work at teaching are to be treated as worthy of double honor. Elsewhere, Paul identifies those who "work hard at preaching and teaching" as gifted "evangelists," "pastors," and "teachers" Christ gives to the Church "for the equipping [preparing] of the saints for the work of service" (Eph. 4:11,12). These gifted men equip God's people for ministry and protect them from doctrinal immaturity and false teaching (Eph. 4:14).

These gifted men "are to be considered worthy of double honor." The imperative verb translated *are to be considered worthy* means "to be rightly deserving" or "to be entitled to" double honor. Paul is not making a suggestion; "double honor" is a requirement, an obligation on the part of each member of the congregation. All who have benefited from the leadership and teaching of such elders are to take the initiative in this practical matter. The point is that certain elders, not all elders, are to receive double honor. This is not meant to create jealousy among elders, but rather is intended to strengthen the eldership and acknowledge that not all elders possess the same giftedness and leading from God.

Regardless of the precise meaning of "double honor," the context makes it clear that material or financial honor is undoubtedly included. 1 Timothy 5:17,18 is part of a larger context in which a series of honor commands appear: "honor" genuine widows (5:3-16), give "double honor" to certain elders (5:17-18), and give "all honor" to nonChristian slave masters (6:1, 2*a*). "Honor" is the key word. In the cases of destitute widows (5:16) and certain elders (5:17), honor includes respect as well as material provision. "All honor" in the case of a slave and his nonChristian master means respect and valuable service. The context determines the differences in nuances of meaning of the word *honor.*

Paul feels so strongly about those who labor in the Word and their rightful entitlement to "double honor" that he immediately backs up his imperative command. In verse 18 he quotes two Scripture passages to bolster his injunction on double honor: "For the Scripture says, 'You shall not muzzle the ox while he is threshing' [Deut. 25:4; 1 Cor. 9:11], and 'The laborer is worthy of his wages [Luke 10:7].'" The hard-working ox must not be denied its share in the harvest; the worker is worthy of his wages; and the laboring elder is worthy of material provision for his needs. This is a New Testament principle of church order and life.

**Not all elders on an elder council are equal in giftedness, effectiveness, influence, time availability, experience, verbal skills, leadership ability, or biblical knowledge.**

These verses from Deuteronomy, Luke, and 1 Corinthians reveal what "double honor" means; namely, material compensation. Similarly, Paul writes in Galatians 6:6: "The one who is taught the word is to share all good things [spiritual and material, Luke 16:25] with the one who teaches him."

Two unbiblical extremes have historically distorted the biblical concept of equality and diversity within the eldership. One extreme is to sacralize and professionalize a gifted elder, making him in effect a Protestant priest: the chief shepherd, the anointed one, or the one who alone can bless, preach, and administer holy things. The other extreme is to force complete equality among the elders, allowing for no special giftedness, calling, function, or financial provision for any member. With God's help, let us seek to represent accurately and completely Christ's instructions on this important subject.

*Appendix B*

# Sample Prayer Guide

**Begin with a time of confession and praise.**

**Pray together for the spiritual life of the church.**

1. Urgent needs

2. Special requests

3. Those who are ill

4. Families and individuals of the church

5. Evangelism

6. Missionaries

7. Those in government, local and national

**Break into small groups for personal requests and needs.**

*Appendix C*

# Sample Agenda

**Date:**

**List Attendees by Name:**

1. **Prayer Time**
2. **Reading and Approval of the Minutes**
   Reading and approval of the minutes reminds everyone of the previous meeting's accomplishments and rallies the group for the work that lies ahead. This is also a time to check on the previous meeting's assignments, providing formal accountability.
3. **Major Discussion Time**
   Organize the agenda so that the largest portion of time is dedicated to discussion of a significant church issue. For example:
   - The spiritual life and vitality of the congregation
   - Vision and future direction of the church
   - Evaluation and direction of the church's overall teaching ministry
   - Sunday school curriculum and philosophy
   - Music ministry
   - Prayer ministry of the church
   - The church's global mission philosophy
   - Local evangelistic outreach
   - Evaluation of the church services
   - Deficiencies of the church
   - Leadership and eldership development
   - Future church planting
   - Assimilation of new people

- The eldership's ministry and needed improvements
- Specific doctrinal issues or problems

4. **Quick Items of Business (approximate time and name of person responsible for each quick item)**

   There are many brief items of business that require a group to make a decision or to give advice, such as setting dates for key events, answering requests from a person or committee, assigning visits or phone calls, delegating an assignment to someone outside the eldership, or solving a problem. This segment of the meeting can include pastoral reports and special announcements.

   Prioritize quick items of business and set a time limit on this segment of the meeting. Don't allow your meetings to become trivialized with mundane work so that you don't get to the significant issues of the church.

   "When agenda items are not prioritized, points of less importance often consume most or all of the time in the meeting, and the most important issues are not given the attention they deserve."[1] If too many quick items are bogging down a meeting, spread them out over several meetings. If a quick item becomes a big item, place it on the list of "Future Discussion Items."

   The "Quick Items" segment of the meeting can be placed before the "Major Discussion" segment, if you prefer. Quick items can also be divided so that a few easy, brief items of business are placed before the major discussion time and several are placed at the end of the major discussion time.

5. **Meeting Summary**

6. **List of Assignments**

   This serves individual participants as well as the group.

7. **Closing Prayer Time**

8. **Future Discussion Items**

   List these items and prioritize them. Doing this allows everyone to see and consider topics for future discussion.

# Endnotes

## Introduction

[1] Lev. 10:1-3.

[2] Mack Tennyson, *Making Committees Work* (Grand Rapids, Mich.: Zondervan, 1992), 20.

## Part One

[1] Tennyson, *Making Committees Work,* 20.

[2] Charles Bridges, *A Modern Study in the Book of Proverbs,* (Milford, Mich.: Mott Media, 1978), 610.

[3] 1 Cor. 4:16; 11:1; Phil. 3:17; 4:9; 1 Thess. 1:6; 2 Thess. 3:9; 2 Tim. 3:10; 1 Peter 5:3.

[4] 1 Thess. 5:11; 2 Thess. 1:2-4; 2 Tim. 1:2,3; Philemon 4,5; Heb. 3:13; 10:26.

[5] Kenneth O. Gangel, *Feeding and Leading* (Wheaton, Ill.: Victor, 1989), 313.

[6] Gangel, *Feeding and Leading,* 309.

[7] A. B. Bruce, *The Training of the Twelve* (1894; Grand Rapids, Mich.: Kregel, 1988), 13.

[8] Bruce Stabbert, *The Team Concept: Paul's Church Leadership Pattern or Ours?* (Tacoma, Wash.: Hegg, 1982), 167.

## Part Two

[1] See Alexander Strauch, *Biblical Eldership: An Urgent Call to Restore Biblical Church Leadership* (Littleton, Colo.: Lewis and Roth, 1995), 195.

[2] Stabbert, *The Team Concept,* 177-81.

[3] Hans Finzel, *The Top Ten Mistakes Leaders Make* (Wheaton, Ill.: Victor Books, 1994), 121.

[4] Kenneth O. Gangel, *Team Leadership in Christian Ministry* (Chicago: Moody Press, 1997), 160.

[5] A. J. Broomhall, *Hudson Taylor and China's Open Century,* 7 vols. Vol. 5: *Refiner's Fire* (London: Hodder and Stoughton, 1985), 342.

[6] Richard N. Longenecker, "Acts," in *The Expositor's Bible Commentary,* 12 vols. (Grand Rapids, Mich.: Zondervan, 1981), 9:289.

[7] Alex Witchel, "Restaurants' Message: No Cell Phones." *The New York Times* (May 5, 1999; Web archives).

[8] Tennyson, *Making Committees Work,* 44.

[9] Derek Kidner suggests that Proverbs 14:23 is "a saying to be framed and hung in council rooms," in *Proverbs,* Tyndale Old Testament Commentaries (Downers Grove, Ill.: InterVarsity, 1964), 47.

[10] Charlie Hawkins, *First Aid for Meetings* (Wilsonville, Ore.: BookPartners, 1997), 131.

[11] Hawkins, *First Aid for Meetings,* 81.

[12] Roger K. Mosvick and Robert B. Nelson, *We've Got to Start Meeting Like This! A Guide to Successful Meeting Management,* revised (Indianapolis: Park Ave. Productions, 1996), 119.

[13] Leon Morris, *The Epistle to the Romans* (Grand Rapids, Mich.: Eerdmans, 1988), 446.

[14] Morris, *The Epistle to the Romans,* 446.

[15] Morris, *The Epistle to the Romans,* 447.

## Appendix A

[1] See Strauch, *Biblical Eldership,* 45-50.

## Appendix C

[1] Hawkins, *First Aid for Meetings,* 45.

# General Index

# Scripture Index



*continued on p. 82*

# Scripture Index

*continued from p. 81*

# Points to Remember before a Meeting

1. **Don't underestimate the significance of your meetings.**

   The elders' meetings are the critical nerve center of the local church body. They have a profound effect on the spiritual health of the church. Meetings refine Christian character, build group morale, provide pastoral accountability, sharpen leadership skills, ignite the power of prayer, and provide a training ground for future elders.

2. **Demonstrate Christlike attitudes and conduct.**

   Sinful attitudes result in unpleasant meetings; Christlike attitudes result in productive, satisfying meetings. Christ's attitude of humility and self-sacrifice should permeate every meeting and shape the attitude of every participant. The new commandment of love sets the standard of conduct for all meetings. Elders are to relate to one another in humility as fellow servants and brothers in Christ.

3. **Take personal responsibility for the meeting's success.**

   Effective meetings result when each participant takes responsibility for a meeting's success, assignments, and decisions. A responsible team member should:

   - Help the group stick to the discussion at hand.
   - Be a good listener and ask for clarification when needed.
   - Express opinions without being an "over-talker."
   - Diligently help the group reach decisions.
   - Accept assignments graciously and follow through on them.

4. **Don't manipulate; rather, speak the truth in love.**

   People who manipulate demean their own character, create distrust among their colleagues, ruin relationships, teach others to manipulate, give Satan a foothold, and open themselves up to further deceit. In contrast, when each participant speaks the truth openly and in love, energy is not wasted worrying about hidden agendas, backroom politicking, or destructive backbiting.

5. **Get the facts before making judgments.**

   When making decisions and when dealing with rumors, accusations, or people problems, it is the elders' responsibility to get all the facts. Determine to give others a fair, honest hearing. Seek by God's grace to be an objective listener and decision maker.

6. **Practice confidentiality.**

   To betray a confidence can ruin an elder's reputation and discredit the entire leadership body. Private statements about people in the church that are made by elders during a meeting must not be shared outside the meeting. An elder should think carefully before sharing confidential information with even his spouse.

7. **Seek to communicate effectively.**

   Be proactive in your communication. Be aware of potential ways you block communication in your meetings. Speak gently, calmly, graciously, and tactfully. Provide adequate instruction when you give someone a job to do. Communicate your decisions to all individuals and groups affected by them. Remember that people need to hear words of encouragement and hear them often.

8. **Be concerned about people.**

   Spend time in your meetings talking about the needs of God's people. Inform one another about newcomers to the church and lost sheep who need to be pursued. Report on recent visits, urgent phone calls, and people who are ill. Periodically invite key leaders of the church to your meetings to exchange information and maintain accountability. The elders' direction and encouragement will help motivate these leaders to persevere and improve their ministries. Returning missionaries also need private time with the elders to share special needs and to seek guidance.

9. **Make prayer a priority.**

   Biblical elders are praying elders. Actively and consistently seek prayer requests from the congregation. Use a meeting prayer guide. Appoint a prayer facilitator. As soon as two people arrive, begin praying. Avoid long, drawn-out prayers; pray shorter prayers. Divide the elders into groups of two for sharing personal needs and praying together for five or ten minutes. Be creative, try new ideas, and continually evaluate the prayer time.

10. **Be focused on God's Word.**

    Elders need to define, clarify, state, and continually restate the church's foundational, nonnegotiable beliefs, unique doctrinal distinctives, ministry priorities, direction, spiritual values, mission, and vision. The elder council thus will have to evaluate and plan its own teaching ministry; define and continually evaluate all major teaching-preaching services; assess and approve all those who teach in the church; set the tone for the way Scripture and doctrine are taught; and plan for evangelism, locally as well as globally.

11. **Strive for effective group facilitation.**

    The role of the facilitator is crucial to productive meetings. A facilitator takes charge of the process of a meeting, but he is not the meeting's boss or sole speaker. Having a facilitator does not exclude other members from actively participating or exercising leadership in the meeting. Different people may facilitate different parts of a meeting. Before jumping to a new topic of discussion, the facilitator should clearly summarize what has been decided, what needs to be done, and by whom.

12. **Follow a well-thought-out agenda.**

    Adequate time spent in preparing an agenda, talking it over with others, thinking it through carefully, prioritizing items, and eliminating needless items guarantees a more productive meeting. Take control of the content of the agenda; ensure that topics crucial to the spiritual health of the church are not ignored. Several times a year, discuss what major topics need to be placed on future agendas. Consider making a special agenda for guiding major discussions, especially complex, hard-to-manage doctrinal discussions. Also, when key ministry leaders meet to consult with the elders, it is usually a good idea to help them prepare an agenda for their discussion.

## 13. Summarize the meeting's accomplishments and assignments.

At the end of the meeting, summarize what has been decided and accomplished. Restate all assignments and who is responsible for the completion of each. The three key questions that always need to be answered are:

- What specifically needs to be done?
- Who is responsible for carrying out the decision?
- When will it be done?

## 14. Keep good records.

The reading of the minutes provides a regular, formal means of checking on the previous meeting's assignments and calls each elder to accountability. The minutes should include the meeting date, names of persons present, key points of discussion, decisions, and follow-up activities. The minutes also should include the names of those responsible for carrying out assignments.

In addition, a notebook should be kept that details all major policy decisions made through the years. This notebook should be at every elders' meeting in case it is needed for reference.

## 15. Delegate, delegate, delegate.

Avoid getting sidetracked on secondary issues, such as building maintenance, and neglecting the responsibilities the New Testament specifically assigns to elders. Delegate as much as possible to others. The work of the local church is to be shared by all its members. If elders teach, organize, and empower the people properly, many within the congregation should be involved in ministering to one another and reaching out to nonbelievers.

## 16. Practice self-evaluation.

Good meetings can get better, and good leaders can become better leaders. Create an atmosphere in which self-evaluation is welcomed, expected, and a normal part of the work. Continually evaluate and look for ways to improve your meetings.

## 17. Make each meeting count.

Few things are as thrilling to a congregation as watching its spiritual leaders grow, learn, and move forward with fresh ideas and vision. Whatever you do as elders, do it to the glory of God, "not lagging behind in diligence, fervent in spirit, serving the Lord" (Rom. 12:11). Ask the One to whom each of us will give an account to help you use the principles in this book to achieve more effective meetings.

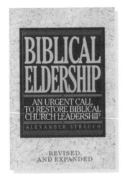

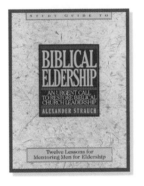

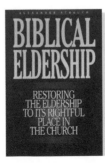

# ADDITIONAL MUST-READ RESOURCES

**Agape Leadership**

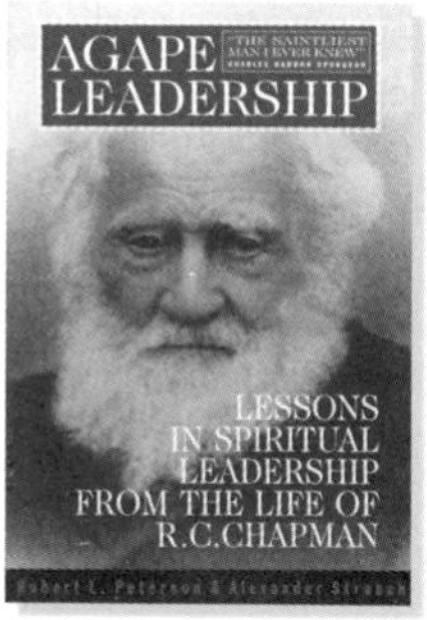


This inspiring biography contains lessons on leadership from the life of R. C. Chapman, a widely respected Christian leader in England during the late 1800s. He was a spiritual mentor to George Müller and a friend of both Hudson Taylor and Charles Haddon Spurgeon. Spurgeon said of Chapman, "He was the saintliest man I ever knew." This book promises to be one of the most spiritually encouraging books you have ever read. It is recommended for all Christians in positions of leadership.

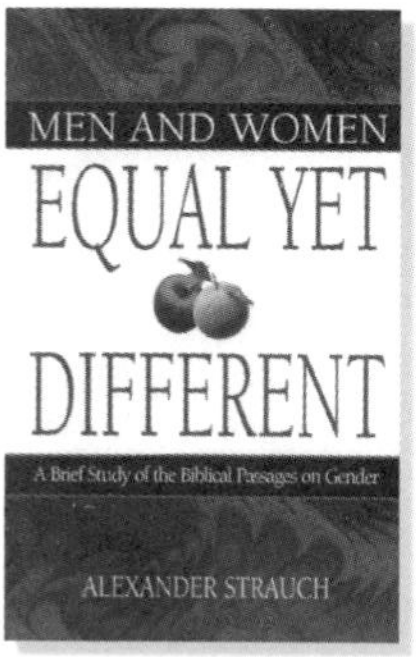


**Men and Women: Equal Yet Different**

Among Bible-believing Christians, intense emotional debate exists over what the Bible says about the roles of men and women. This book provides a much-needed introduction to the key terms, arguments, Scripture passages, and new research related to the complementarian (non-feminist) position on gender. It also presents the biblical evidence that men and women are created equal, yet have been given different gender-specific roles to fulfill in the family and in the church.

"Alexander Strauch has courageously not caved in to the pressures from contemporary culture or misguided evangelicals to become a 'gender blender...' "

—***John MacArthur Jr.***
*Pastor-Teacher, President, The Master's College*

"... *Men and Women: Equal Yet Different* lets the Bible speak for itself in the clearest of terms."

—***R. Kent Hughes***
*Pastor, College Church, Wheaton, Ill.*

"[This] volume is strategically important. [It] gives an introduction to the subject that offers clear and easily understood information for the lay person as well as challenging considerations for the scholar." —***Dorothy Kelley Patterson***
*Assistant Professor of Women's Studies, Southeastern Baptist Theological Seminary*

"This book is one of the best investments of time and money on one of the most important issues of our day—and of any time. Take, read, feed your minds, clear your heads, and rejoice in and live out God's truth."

—***Dr. George W. Knight III***
*Former New Testament Professor at Knox Theological Seminary and author of "The Pastoral Epistles" in* The New International Greek Commentary

"[A] welcome study of the important subject of gender roles. It is biblically sound and clearly written. It should be read by everyone who is seriously concerned about the future of the church." —***Jack Cottrell, Ph.D.***
*Professor of Theology, Cincinnati Bible College and Seminary*